PRAISE FOR
THE PEOPLE FORMULA

"Jane Sunley tells it like it is in The People Formula. It's a jargon-free zone. The book is full of step-by-step guides and practical approaches to dealing with the most pressing people issues organisations face today, backed up with real-life case studies and data."

JO FARAGHER, HR JOURNALIST OF THE YEAR 2015

"This book charts the path for HR Management 2.0. A fantastic book for addressing the current business challenges and redefining the role of the HR function."

PROFESSOR VLATKA HLUPIC, AUTHOR OF AWARD-WINNING BOOK *THE MANAGEMENT SHIFT*, INCLUDED IN MOST INFLUENTIAL INTERNATIONAL HR THINKERS LIST 2015

"With so many books analysing the complex theory of HR, I have been waiting for one on people centric leadership, which cuts through the noise and gives readers practical advice they can use straight away. In The People Formula Jane Sunley uses her own brand of common sense know-how to prove that through simple, powerful and easy-to-apply solutions, business success is only 12 steps away. This is backed up with a wealth of business-savvy anecdotes, case studies and examples from leaders in some well-known global brands - as well as up and coming start-ups with innovative ideas. The People Formula *is a straight forward and welcome read for busy executives. Its layout, top 10 tips and takeaways at the end of each chapter, make it easy for readers to apply the learnings directly into real time practical applications, at the front line of business strategy.* "

EUGENIO PIRRI, VICE PRESIDENT, PEOPLE & ORGANISATIONAL DEVELOPMENT, DORCHESTER COLLECTION AND HR DIRECTOR OF THE YEAR, 2014

"*Jane Sunley has always known that 'the people stuff' is a fundamental component of business success - and in* The People Formula *she's been able to cleverly show how anyone in business can generate positive long term results through her straightforward plan of action for HR. The raft of case studies and success stories will help you prove this to even the most cynical colleagues! There's something in this practical and entertaining book for everyone - from small business owner to corporate HR director and CEO.*"

TEA COLAIANNI, GROUP HR DIRECTOR, MERLIN ENTERTAINMENTS GROUP

"In an age where attraction and retention of staff is already a challenge, engaging enabling and empowering employees, once they are on board, is paramount. This book maps a clear path through the myriad of challenges faced by organisations in our present day and offers insight and innovation into the 'people stuff'. Jane has an amazing ability to 'uncomplicate' things, which resonates loudly with me and made me want to read on. This is a fantastic and very useful book for anyone with people management responsibility."

MELISSA BOYD, HUMAN RESOURCES DIRECTOR, THOMAS SABO

"If we, as people and leaders, can deliver on what our fellow colleagues, friends and family really want from us, we will be strengthening relationships. And strong relationships, where people are safe, trusted and respected, lead to strong organisations that can successfully ride above the waves and travel to a brighter tomorrow. The People Formula not only illuminates the things that make successful relationships and organisations function, but provides the working tools and immediate actionable insights to start building and improving those relationships today."

MOE GLENNER, CONSULTANT AND AUTHOR OF *+CHANGE: GENESIS OF INNOVATION AND SELFISH ALTRUISM: MANAGING AND EXECUTING SUCCESSFUL CHANGE INITIATIVES*

For Jo
and the Purple People

THE
PEOPLE
FORMULA

12 STEPS TO PRODUCTIVE, PROFITABLE, PERFORMING BUSINESS

Published by

Humm Publishing

Part of Humm Media Limited
Union House,
20 Kentish Town Road,
London, NW1 9NX

hello@hummmedia.com
www.hummmedia.com

© Jane Sunley 2016
© Humm Publishing 2016

ISBN: 978-0-9934271-0-7

Printed in Great Britain by TJ International
Cover and page design: Laura Hawkins

THE
PEOPLE
FORMULA

12 STEPS TO PRODUCTIVE, PROFITABLE, PERFORMING BUSINESS

JANE SUNLEY

To the brilliant business and thought leaders
quoted throughout this book, who were so frank
and generous with their information

To my colleagues for allowing me the luxury
of time to think and write

To everyone who enjoyed my previous books
and showed there's an appetite for this one

To Humm Publishing for being
marvellous in every way

CONTENTS

Part one

THE

ALLENGE

*m*aybe you're a CEO, a CFO, a business owner, a head of people (in one of its many guises), an operational leader, a line manager, a marketer or are generally interested in the wonderful and very valuable asset that is 'human resources'?

If so, you'll know that only by engaging, enabling and empowering an organisation's people, can true competitive advantage be achieved in business. You'll also know that the world has never been more volatile, less certain, more complex or more fraught with ambiguity than it is today.

When it comes to 'the people stuff', business leaders still tend to overcomplicate the issue, engaging in a silo mentality, implementing 'tick box strategies', and consigning much needed action to the 'too difficult' box. In some cases those responsible for people strategy don't believe they have, or are unable to argue persuasively for, the essential resource needed to bring about the required change.

Why? Because, even in the 21st century, so many of those accountable for 'the people stuff' are still stuck with 'the old ways' of operating, some of which were designed as far back as the industrial revolution; most, long before many of today's working population were even born, years before the advent of technology as we know it. This is an unwelcome hangover from the time when manufacturing trumped service and when leadership was based on autocracy; when overdone process overruled common sense.

EVEN THE MOST SAVVY 'PEOPLE PEOPLE' ARE DROWNING IN SWATHES OF POLICIES

As a result, even the most savvy 'people people' are drowning in swathes of policies, tied up in compliance and legislative matters, desperately trying to make the numbers work without the right tools to do the job they're actually there to do.

If we look at the falling productivity levels of UK plc, this approach is clearly not working and, if we're being direct about it, business as we know it is, in far too many instances, just not cutting it:

★ Gallup's 2015 global workplace study, across 142 countries, revealed that only 13% of the working population does much more than show up on time and meet the minimum expectations for their jobs…

★ The *Deloitte 2015 Global Human Capital Trends* report stated that the gap is widening between what business leaders want and what

HR is delivering. Engagement and culture have skyrocketed to their number one issue around the world (87% of companies rated it important or very important). Yet Deloitte's research with employer ratings website Glassdoor, showed that only half of all employees would recommend their employer to their friends...

★ The UK Investors in People's 2015 *Jobs exodus trends* employee sentiment poll, found 65% of employees are not happy in their role – meaning companies need to work harder at engaging and retaining their talent, and also at attracting talent from elsewhere...

The Deloitte report also makes the case for a new HR playbook – one that taps HR to be more agile, forward thinking, and bolder in its solutions.

The People Formula sets out to achieve this by:
★ providing the 'how' for people leaders

★ bridging the gap between academic thought and real-world use

★ being incredibly practical, written in a language that is easy to understand

★ packing in plenty of do-able, uncommon, common sense advice which can be actioned immediately

★ providing techniques and examples that are workable within any size or sector of business.

If you don't have a dedicated HR resource, then this book is great for you too. I very much believe in the business case for helping transition HR from 'doing' to 'facilitating' – to becoming a business-savvy, business driver – and you're halfway there already. Who doesn't want their organisation to be as successful and durable as possible?

Who knows what the next 10 - 20 years will bring? What will talent management 'look like' in the future?

What is certain is that businesses will always need talented people, and attracting, engaging, developing and retaining them is a business challenge that is becoming more important.

In writing this book, I've talked to some of the UK's most successful HR directors, CEOs, entrepreneurs and innovators from organisations large and small, incorporating some of their suggestions so you can see, first-hand, 'how it's done'.

DON'T JUST TAKE IT FROM ME

"I think we can expect more volatility. Organisations face new challenges every day. The explosion of technology has changed how we manage and an influx of millennials and knowledge workers into organisations means these staff don't want to be micromanaged – they're looking for meaning, purpose and coaching."

VLATKA HLUPIC, PROFESSOR OF BUSINESS AND MANAGEMENT, UNIVERSITY OF WESTMINSTER

"The workplace has changed enormously and has become a more ethereal thing for employees. People want a career in multiple places and are prepared to take jobs for the experience and to have a story for their CV. The repercussions mean employers have to ask themselves:

'Why would people want to work here? What's in it for them?'

"There is a competition for talent and small businesses like ours in the digital sector are competing for talent with startups, rapidly growing businesses like Facebook, as well as corporates such as investment banks. We're competing on a world stage – there is no local labour market, so we have to be a desirable place to work.

Employers can't fool employees anymore; if they're not able to pay as much as competitors, they have to know what they can give staff that other employers can't."

TIM MORGAN, CEO, MINT DIGITAL

"The big question on everyone's lips is what jobs will be like in 10 or 20 years. The exponential revolution going on in technology is disrupting businesses faster than organisations can plan for, never mind that regulation can be brought up to date for! Once we work that out, the biggest challenges will be the same as today…"

ISABEL NAIDOO, VICE PRESIDENT HUMAN RESOURCES, FIS GLOBAL

"It's difficult to forecast and estimate for the future. I think technology will affect working patterns. Millennials are coming into workplaces and they have a new view, which is different from baby boomers and generation X.

"It's a volatile marketplace, commodities are being devalued and it's impossible to predict. Also there are geo-political factors such as the rise of radical Islam and relocation of people across Europe that will have an impact on the workplace of the future. These will challenge traditional workplace hierarchies and lead to upheaval."

GARETH HUGHES, MANAGING DIRECTOR AND HEAD OF HR (EUROPE), ROYAL BANK OF CANADA CAPITAL MARKETS

IF YOU ONLY DO
three things:

1. **READ THIS BOOK WITH AN OPEN AND EAGER MIND.**

2. **THINK ABOUT IT, SCRIBBLE ON IT, STEAL THE IDEAS IN IT.**

3. **BE PREPARED TO TAKE ACTION AND MAKE CHANGE HAPPEN.**

Notes...

....

....

....

....

....

....

THE BIGGER PICTURE

Put simply, I know that business success is truly dependent upon three key I's:

1. **Ideas:** compelling innovations, around which you can create an easily marketable brand

2. **Investment:** capital for startup and growth plus cash flow; the life-blood of every organisation

3. **Individuals:** the right talented people, in the right roles, delivering innovation and high levels of service, realising their potential – in a happy, healthy and inspired way.

These three are of equal importance; yet the third 'I' is rarely given the attention, time, resourcing and investment it needs or deserves. There is a massive gulf between recognising the power of people and delivering a robust people strategy in our fast-moving, ever-more demanding and diverse world.

Becoming people-centric is the way to go.

I love meeting courageous, determined and high-impact heads of people/chief people officers (CPOs) who have positioned themselves in a triangular relationship with the CEO and CFO. This is the way to get things done, secure the necessary investment and create commitment from the very top.

Yet I also know people-centricity can be achieved by anyone and everyone. And this lies at the crux of the matter. HR departments cannot be solely responsible for the third 'I' – it's a team job; one in which everyone, in every organisation, has to play their part, from the guy sweeping the corridor to the chairman of the board.

By understanding how to join up the people stuff into a clear, straightforward strategy, any organisation can build a robust and actionable plan that will transform it, with measurable and profitable results to boot.

There's a great (true) story about a managing director who pitched the idea of recruiting a global HR director (HRD) for the first time, to his board of directors only to discover they thought they already had one! This shows that:

a) *the board wasn't giving much board room time to the third 'I'*

b) *the expectations of said HRD must have been pretty low.*

I know this from the person who was ultimately appointed to the role and who went on to take the organisation by storm. The board certainly knows it has a group HRD now.

I've seen very successful small and medium enterprises (SMEs) that employ no internal HR resource at all, turning over tens of millions of pounds and winning prestigious people awards along the way. This is achievable because the founders have set a clear direction and tone for the people stuff and they – and their employees – all know their part to play. What a great model for getting this stuff right.

FIGHTING TO SURVIVE

So why does the people stuff fall by the wayside of good intention so often if it's so important?

The answer is worryingly simple – because many business leaders and owners are often too busy dealing with the business of day to day. They're fighting to survive and thrive, and in doing so, allow the subject of people to fall off the bottom of their ever-growing to-do lists. Consequently, people become disengaged, dropping in and out of the organisation at an alarming rate, costing time, hassle and money. Most organisations don't measure the cost of replacing a leaver – it's just too difficult, too scary or both. Is it any wonder they're fighting for said survival?

In case you're not convinced (or someone you know isn't – yet), I'm going to lay out these costs for you in black and white. For a start, there are the direct costs of recruiting a replacement (recruitment fees, time, interim cover, induction and so on). The big impact though, is made by the indirect costs – the expenditure business leaders often don't even pause to consider (see step 10).

These include:

★ knowledge loss

★ general instability

★ service disruption/quality

★ customer relationships/loss

★ increased threat of competition

★ other people leaving

★ drop in productivity

★ effect on morale

★ disruption to team dynamic

★ effects on reputation.

You can probably come up with lots more if you really think about it…

So why isn't anyone doing anything about it?

Again, the answer is not earth-shattering. Put simply, growth organisations and their leaders do not make the time or allow the resource needed to deliver on the people stuff, even though they know they should.

The research speaks for itself:

★ 100% of business leaders say you need a people plan

★ 98% say developing people is vital

★ 90% are convinced that people create competitive advantage

Yet:

★ 86% admit to not having a consistent people plan

★ 85% say managing people development that supports business growth is a challenge

★ 70% state time and finance as barriers

Source: Purple Cubed with networks associated with Cranfield Business School and Lancaster Management University

While it's encouraging that so many organisations recognise getting the 'people stuff' right is the key to achieving objectives, it's also shocking that there's such a notable shortfall when it comes to actually delivering on it. Some people have told me it's just too difficult. Too big a task. There are other priorities. Others say it's impossible to get buy-in from the top. There isn't the budget. We don't have the people to do it. Yada, yada, it goes on…

Well, the majority of organisations depend on people to make them successful; harnessing the power of individuals to help deliver business success and growth is not an optional extra. It is a business imperative.

In many businesses the connection between people and profit quite simply is not being made, as corporates battle to put plans in place to reach their targets. Why aren't the people analytics reported within the annual report as with other key metrics? Why is 'people' not top of the agenda at the board or business meeting?

THE MAJORITY OF ORGANISATIONS DEPEND ON PEOPLE TO MAKE THEM SUCCESSFUL.

Although becoming people-centric can't, and won't, happen in every organisation overnight, the journey has to start somewhere.

By breaking down the important stuff into manageable chunks, it really is possible to achieve and definitely worth the effort. As you become more focused on your people and their progression you will, no doubt about it, reap the benefits of an inspired, developing workforce which has the skills and personalities to progress the organisation further and achieve greater (and ever greater) business success. So start small and build…

And for the organisations that succeed in this (and they are the ones at the top of the 'fastest-growing' or 'most successful organisation' lists making super-profits as they go), they should strive to be strong in all of the areas of *The People Formula: 12 steps to productive, profitable and performing businesses.*

Notes…

....

....

....

....

....

THE PEOPLE FORMULA

STEP

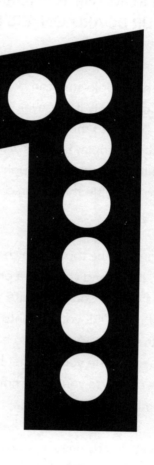

STEP 1

BUY-IN FROM THE TOP (OR HOW TO GET YOUR BOARD ON, ER, BOARD)

*T*he people stuff can only be delivered effectively if whoever holds the power buys into the idea of achieving profit through their people. Leaders will need to be prepared to support you throughout, especially by making available the required investment to get this right.

Maybe you are 'the top', in which case this step is an easy one. If not, and you're in a position where those in the boardroom don't yet quite 'get it', you have work to do BEFORE you dive into any of the other steps in this book. My advice to heads of people is always to negotiate your budget before accepting the role – of course you might not be in that position (so remember it for next time).

If you don't already have a people-centric CEO, MD, owner, or other person of power, then you might only have one shot at engaging them in this journey.

You simply cannot afford to mess it up by being ill-prepared, unclear or fluffy about this – this has been the downfall of too many HR directors, who now find themselves up to their eyeballs in operational HR, while their inspirational and transformational people strategy gathers dust in a corner.

Money talks… and so do numbers; you have to be able to prove your business case as you would in any other discipline within an organisation. Your sales director didn't get sign-off for that expensive new database without illustrating the business benefits it will bring.

So, do your homework, be business savvy in your approach; know your stuff. When presenting your business case keep it SIMPLE – your goal is to excite, engage and enthuse your fellow directors/colleagues/boss/board (not bore them to death).

When presenting this type of stuff, think like them. Talk their language. What do they need to know to support this decision? It's important to stick to the facts (while resisting the urge to become carried away by your own excitement). If that sounds patronising, it's not meant to be. I see this sort of stuff happening every day and it is holding 'team HR' back.

ALWAYS START WITH THE 'WHY'

Too many people dive into the 'what' (strategy) and the 'how' (tactics) first. So colleagues may well become excited in the short term. However, without context (the 'why' – setting the scene), and the benefits (the 'what if') the enthusiasm soon peters out and everyone moves onto the next big thing.

This is why so many 'initiatives' fail. (Initiatives are not a very good idea – if we're looking at the big picture, the longer term, then this is a culture change; a new way of life, joined-up steps and stages on a journey – far more than a series of 'initiatives'.)

This book is not all about research – it's a practical guide to achieving productive, profitable, performing business. However, you have to start with hard evidence to be able to progress this and thus make a difference. And remember, you do have access to every piece of knowledge ever written, right there in the palm of your hand – so use it and use it wisely.

YOU HAVE TO START WITH HARD EVIDENCE TO BE ABLE TO MAKE A DIFFERENCE...

Below are just a few simple examples of 'ammunition', found at the time of writing, with which to persuade, cajole, negotiate or otherwise sell the idea to the relevant parties.

A few good reasons your board should sit up and listen:

★ Companies with low engagement scores earned an operating income 32.7% lower than companies with more engaged employees.

★ Companies with a highly engaged workforce experienced a 19.2% growth in operating income over a 12-month period.

Source: Engaging for Success: enhancing performance through employee engagement - *prepared for the UK government, David MacLeod and Nita Clarke*

★ Engaged companies grow profits up to three times faster than their competitors.

★ Highly engaged employees are 87% less likely to leave the organisation.

Source: Corporate Leadership Council *study of engagement levels of 50,000 employees globally*

★ A disengaged employee costs an organisation approximately $3,400 for every $10,000 in annual salary.

★ Disengaged employees cost the US economy up to $350 billion per year due to lost productivity.

Source: McLean & Company

And, of course, by becoming a great place in which to work, your organisation will:

★ attract great talent, retaining it longer than you do now

★ by improving engagement, you will also boost productivity, innovation and profits (for your CFO or FD) and save money

★ win some awards thus improving your profile with clients and employees

★ increase brand value and image.

First, though, you'll probably be required to prove it…

DON'T JUST TAKE IT FROM ME

"If you're lucky enough to work with a CEO who gets it like I do, there is little to be done to get folks on board. But if you don't, then go back to basics – cite the facts, commit to measurement, shout about your achievements and impacts and find other influencers who can speak to their experiences."

ISABEL NAIDOO, VICE PRESIDENT HUMAN RESOURCES, FIS GLOBAL

"The value of people has to be shown to be proportional to key objectives and cost. We can show that to our board pretty well at EE and I think this is why HR is given air time at the top table."

ROBERT PURDY, DIRECTOR OF IT, CUSTOMER MANAGEMENT AND DELIVERY, EE

"The CEO and the board must have the appetite for people-centric ideas – without that, you are unlikely to succeed. Once you have a supportive senior leadership team, the HR function should outline a clear strategy and plan to deliver – linked to the business agenda throughout. Get buy-in and non-HR sponsorship for projects, then involve as many people as you can to ensure that you stress-test the execution of your initiatives."

ALAN MELLOR, HEAD OF EMPLOYEE ENGAGEMENT, PENTLAND BRANDS

IF YOU ONLY DO
three things:

1. **DO YOUR HOMEWORK; KNOW YOUR STUFF.**

2. **PRESENT A SHORT, SHARP, COMPELLING BUSINESS CASE.**

3. **START SIMPLY; PROVE THIS STUFF WORKS.**

Notes...

....

....

....

....

....

....

....

....

....

....

....

....

....

....

....

....

....

....

....

....

STEP

STEP 2
CULTURE AND VALUES

Visions, missions, culture and values are what your organisation stands for.

Mission and vision provide the 'why', if you like – why you're in business; why you do what you do and where you're going with it. You don't even have to use these standard terms. You could just say: "This is what we're about. This is what we stand for. This is where we're headed."

It's vital that every single team member and potential team member can easily understand what you're all about; what you stand for; and where you're going. Most importantly, this message needs to be consistent throughout the organisation.

The important thing is that you and your leadership team are able to articulate clearly what you stand for and that everyone within your organisation understands that too. And through your values (see page 46), know how it relates to each employee and his or her role.

This is a big ask, but you absolutely need to get it right before you do anything else. It will be the glue that connects the 12 steps, keeping parity throughout the ups and downs, swings and roundabouts and constant change of business as it is today.

KEEP IT SIMPLE AND MEMORABLE

Long mission and/or vision statements that no one, not even the CEO, can remember, are a really bad idea. You'd be surprised by the number of well-respected companies that believe everyone knows their vision, and then when you ask a) the receptionist b) the department head c) the CEO, none of them will be able to tell you.

I know, because I test this out all the time. I was once discussing the clarity of company purpose and values with a CEO and his HR director. "Oh," he said with a rather self-satisfied smirk. "We got all *that* stuff sorted out ages ago."

So I asked what their mission and vision statement were. And of course, neither of them knew. The HR director shuffled about uncomfortably, delving into his briefcase for his credit card-sized reminder, though couldn't find it. Then the CEO called through to his assistant, who didn't know either. I'd also asked the receptionist on the way in who didn't have a clue what I was talking about. By now, the HR director had turned a nasty shade of puce and had started to mumble apologetically. The CEO didn't understand that he was the one who should have been shouting this stuff from the rafters. I guess that's because he probably believed it to be an 'HR initiative'…

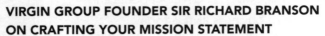

VIRGIN GROUP FOUNDER SIR RICHARD BRANSON ON CRAFTING YOUR MISSION STATEMENT

"Brevity is certainly key, so try using Twitter's 140-character template when you're drafting your inspirational message. You need to explain your company's purpose and outline expectations for internal and external clients alike. Make it unique to your company, make it memorable, keep it real and, just for fun, imagine it on the bottom of a coat of arms."

Accordingly, Virgin Atlantic's mission is: "To embrace the human spirit and let it fly."

That's 42 characters – nice job Sir Richard!

Another example, from Google: *"To organize the world's information and make it universally accessible and useful."*

So if you're building a mission statement, make it as simple, as visible and as memorable as possible. That way, you can really make it live. Getting it down to a clear and simple message is really hard to do and if you're struggling with making it simple, bring in some expertise to help you work through the options (giving them a 140-character limit, because some experts over-complicate the process as well)!

ARTICULATE YOUR VALUES

It's also necessary to articulate your 'values'; what your organisation stands for; how you go about your day-to-day business. This is very important to today's employee who seeks meaning from work.

Values should be simple enough to remember so they can be properly and easily embedded. They are the thread which runs through everything you do.

Up to five is a good, manageable number of values. Mnemonics and acronyms are very useful for helping people remember. For example, childcare provider Bright Horizons Family Solutions uses HEART – honesty, excellence, accountability, respect and teamwork.

If you haven't yet defined your values it's important to do this properly. To save time, let the board determine these (they might need some facilitation). And then work hard on it with the rest of the organisation.

I realise inclusivity is key, but consulting everyone is going to take a really long time and the strong 'essence' of what you are will become diluted. If you want to move fast (and in today's business you need to) you can't afford to make every decision by consensus. The important thing is to communicate really well, involve people in the execution and work with them to gain real buy-in.

Harvard Business School Professor, Howard Stevenson, concurs, saying that: "maintaining an effective culture is so important that it trumps even strategy." This means that existing leaders and employees must decide upon, support and deliver on the desired cultural norms and parameters – together.

Perhaps, then, it is the job of a really great performer to understand, live and breathe the values, and to evolve them. It's also about mutual trust and respect between employees and their leaders; being able to have an honest, two-way conversation in order to drive the business towards cultural success.

The important thing is to ensure leaders are really getting to grips with their culture and communicating with their people; understanding the way they work as individuals and how they interpret the values; and helping them to get it right through role-model behaviour, high standards and support. Then it's a matter of delivering it, over and over again...

If you can find a way to make sure people actually remember your values, relate to them, like them and feel proud – they can truly live them every day. Talk about your values all the time. Consider the values in every decision you make. If something doesn't fit the values, whether that's a person, potential client or internal communication, then you'll know it's not right to progress further.

In most cases, it's unusual for someone to be able to thrive and survive within your organisation if they don't 'get' what you're about. This is particularly true of organisations in which customer service is key to growth and where people can make or break the brand.

You should also review your values annually to make sure they are still absolutely relevant and true for your organisation. HOWEVER resist the need to change them unless ABSOLUTELY necessary. Changing firmly embedded values is even harder than changing your brand identity. This is why culture change is such a challenging thing.

This stuff only works if you get it right, feed it every day and then stop mucking about with it. This is your culture you're talking about, you should leave well alone unless it's broken and your remit is to change it.

A 10-POINT, FOOL-PROOF METHOD FOR EMBEDDING YOUR VALUES

1. Avoid the archetypal 'road-show' or PowerPoint presentation. (That old adage: "I hear; I forget. I see; I remember. I do; I understand," has never been truer.)

2. Instead, develop line-managers and others to work with their teams to determine:

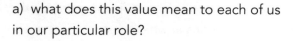
a) what does this value mean to each of us in our particular role?

b) how will we know we're doing it?

(This is a facilitated discussion around practical examples. So, if one of your values is 'achievement', for one person it might be completing everything on the day's schedule, for another it will be meeting the target EBITDA (earnings before interest, taxes, depreciation and amortization); for another, 'landing the plane' safely.)

3. Incorporate your values into daily language; for this example, ask: "Will this help us achieve the goal?"

4. Make sure values are visible too. Some people put their values on posters or credit card-sized reminders, which is a start, though not a substitute for knowing and living them. Certainly, they must be on your website and on appropriate collateral; I also like to see them in well-used places such as on the back of toilet doors or by the coffee machine. (Don't overdo it though – you're not a cult!)

5. Use values in recruitment: expect every candidate to be familiar with them from their research. Ask prospective employees how they feel they could relate the values of the company to the role on offer. Look them in the eye and ask whether they can give 100% commitment to upholding these values.

6. Use your values in inductions, day to day, in meetings, in the board room.

7. Measure people's performance against the values.

8. Incorporate the values in all learning and development activity.

9. Use values in planning, briefings and team meetings to keep them alive and kicking.

10. And most importantly, leaders (at all levels) must live your values every day and NEVER (ever) compromise them (and if they do, they must own up fast and fix it faster).

DON'T JUST TAKE IT FROM ME

"It's so important to create a strong and recognisable culture. This is not about having printed collateral and so on, it's about keeping the message simple. It's about making sure that everyone, from the highest level down 'lives it' on a continuous basis.

"Talk about culture in the decisions you make, measure

potential recruits against it - if they can't live it then don't employ them. You have to imprint it upon everyone who's involved. That's what makes a business stand out from the rest; enabling growth and success.

"When a company is small, the culture permeates naturally, but as they grow it becomes more difficult to ensure the message doesn't become diluted. So when the company gets bigger, it's crucial that, on a daily basis, every message and every direction given by a leader to their teams must contain the essence of the company culture. This can be achieved through formal communications or informal, ad hoc conversations.

"Leaders and others have to give culture the attention it deserves: feed it, nurture it and promote it - every day, day in, day out."

MARTIN KUCZMARSKI, CHIEF OPERATION OFFICER, SOHO HOUSE & CO

"I firmly believe that in any business, regardless of shape, size and sector, skills can be taught. But appreciation and love for a company culture is something that can never be put upon someone – it's something that people just have.

"My advice for keeping the cultural fire burning in a business, is to think every day about the authentic things that make your company great – or just unique. Keep these values at the heart of every

business decision you make and ask yourself, if you make a tough choice that doesn't fit in with your values – no matter how much pressure you feel - if this is the right decision for the business.

"It's culture and authenticity that gives a business a USP and the impetus for growth – you generate custom and attract talent through a great culture and that strengthens the argument for keeping your culture at the heart of business development. Remember this golden rule and a conflict of culture versus growth should never arise."

MIKE WILLIAMS, PEOPLE DIRECTOR, BYRON HAMBURGERS

"When it comes to the company culture, it starts with the individual. At Metro Bank, it's about feeling cared for and connecting with a customer who walks out smiling, or about a person you hired getting a promotion. Everything you do makes up culture and you have to be passionate and fanatical about it. For example, we have disciplinary and grievance policy that says: 'If you're reading this you're having a difficult time at work.' It's more human in tone and the procedure is far more mature - we ask that at first you try to sort it out because we're all grown up. This empowers the person once again."

DANIELLE HARMER, CHIEF PEOPLE OFFICER, METRO BANK

IF YOU ONLY DO
three things:

1. **KEEP IT SIMPLE AND MEMORABLE.**

2. **LEADERS AND CHAMPIONS MUST LIVE THE MESSAGE – ALWAYS.**

3. **FEED YOUR VALUES DAILY TO KEEP THEM ALIVE.**

Notes...

....

....

....

....

....

....

STEP

STEP 3
DIGITISING AND SOCIALISING HR

*T*alent has gone digital – even great-grandparents are Skyping, texting, tweeting and checking into Facebook.

Yet the HR world hasn't followed suit.

If the baby boomers and even 'the veterans' are doing it why aren't contemporary HR professionals joining in? According to Cap Gemini, 75% of leaders in HR and talent management say their companies are behind the curve in the use of internal and social networking sites.

It might be that they don't have the profile or the proficiency to argue persuasively for investment. Perhaps they're risk averse; frightened of 'getting it wrong'? Perhaps they're so afraid of making mistakes that they're completely bypassing the potential opportunities? Maybe they're so bogged down in day-to-day administrative compliance and policy issues that they just haven't made the time to think about it.

Many HR professionals are afraid to raise their heads above the parapet and rock the boat. The cliché goes that no one ever lost his or her job by not rocking the boat. Well, pretty soon they may find themselves looking for a new job if they don't take action. It is time to bring HR firmly and determinedly into the 21st century.

Imagine completing the monthly payroll manually. That's the past. Conversely, imagine the talent review being as easy as using your favourite social network. That's tomorrow. It's going to happen, so you may as well embrace it. Some people have already taken this leap – though far too few. It's failing to move with the times like this that's setting HR way behind the curve.

The business case is clear and acting now will create competitive advantage. There is plenty of compelling evidence out there. For example, according to Cap Gemini (US 2013/14):

★ mobile devices now account for one billion job searches every year, and counting

★ only 6% of organisations use social recruitment

★ a staggering 80% of organisations still rely on one-way communications tools for learning and development

★ gamification improves the embedding of learning by 40%

★ more than half (56%) of employers lack any kind of measures for talent investment returns

Meanwhile:

★ Logistics company UPS saw hires from mobile/social recruitment go from 19 to more than 15,000 in the past three years

★ UK hospitality company, De Vere Hotels and Village Urban Resorts, invested in HR technology and added £3m to their EBITDA

"TALENT MANAGEMENT" IS ABOUT ATTRACTING, IDENTIFYING, ENGAGING, DEVELOPING, PROGRESSING AND RETAINING YOUR PEOPLE, MAKING USE OF THEIR SKILLS AND KNOWLEDGE IN THE BEST WAY FOR BOTH INDIVIDUAL AND ORGANISATION.

RECRUIT DIGITAL NATIVES

Embracing social technology doesn't have to involve a high level of investment; it does, however, need people with the skills to understand, embrace and deliver on it. There are thousands of graduates and school leavers out there with these skills (they're digital natives), so work out what needs to be done, start simply and make it happen.

Systems for talent management and analytics will require more investment, so it's important to be able to build a sound business case.

If 'talent' is your workforce (i.e. the right people for the organisation who can make a great contribution and have the potential to keep doing so), 'talent management' is about attracting, identifying, engaging, developing, progressing and retaining said talent, making use of their skills and knowledge in the best way for both individual and organisation. A talent management system will therefore help you to do this by digitising the processes and bringing about a bottom-up approach.

More and more systems are beginning to 'talk' to one another and it's still very difficult to find any one system that can do everything to the standard you require. It may be necessary to shop around, connecting different software to achieve the whole picture.

According to Deloitte: "Core human resources management systems and talent management features (e.g. payroll, performance management, recruiting, learning management, and succession management) are available from most major providers. But the exciting new tools (e.g. social and informal learning, integrated network recruiting and candidate relationship management, social recognition, real-time employee feedback and engagement sensing, culture assessment and fit analysis, and many others) are usually only available from small, innovative vendors. So, as you firm up your core system of record into a single enterprise resource-planning suite, you may also find yourself wanting to buy innovative tools from smaller vendors as well."

So remember one size doesn't fit all – you might need to shop around.

A 10-POINT PLAN FOR APPROACHING INVESTMENT IN HR TECHNOLOGY:

1. Look at the big picture, clearly identify the issues to be fixed and know your stuff.

2. Build your business case using hard measures such as ROI and softer ones, such as effect on culture.

3. Think about the stakeholders; work out how to engage them.

4. Craft a strategic solution.

5. Phase your approach, starting simply to prove it works (ideally bring evidence of the ROI on some low-cost stuff you've already done).

6. Build in milestones and metrics.

7. Gather evidence: facts and figures, likely outcomes, case studies (including completion stats – you want to know people will use it)

8. Pick the right time.

9. Lobby for top-down consensus and support informally.

10. Present your case accordingly, making it short, sharp and business savvy.

....

DON'T JUST TAKE IT FROM ME

CASE STUDY:
DE VERE HOTELS & VILLAGE URBAN RESORTS

De Vere Hotels & Village Urban Resorts is a UK-based hotel chain with 33 properties and more than 5,000 employees at the time of writing. It has an annual turnover of £220m and £60m EBITDA, with an HR team of (just) seven.

Previously, there was little focus on, or investment in, people at De Vere Hotels and Village Urban Resorts. However, when a visionary new CEO and an HR director were recruited in 2012, with a remit to grow the business and boost financial revenue, this approach quickly changed.

A new people plan was created and prioritised on the board agenda, ensuring that people were placed at the heart of business strategy. The focus of this strategy was the combination of brand and technology. 'V Happy People' was introduced and launched via a social communications hub, which ensured people felt a sense of connection with the brand as a whole and were able to engage in two-way communication with the business, both inside and out of work.

Sitting alongside the communications hub was an automated performance and talent management tool which empowered people to drive their own goals and careers.

In just one year, the businesses were able to add £3m to their EBITDA; create a robust internal talent pipeline which resulted in a £400K saving on recruitment fees; achieve cost savings through greater transparency and collecting innovative employee ideas (one idea alone generated £500k per annum in savings); reduce labour turnover by 57%; and increase unsolicited job applications by 16%.

Former CEO Robert Cook, says: *"We needed a phenomenal way of measuring talent in our business. We could only grow as quickly as talent was available and therefore having a pulse on this situation makes it credible. Automating our talent management, making the right changes around that completely transformed our organisation."*

IF YOU ONLY DO *three things:*

1. **RESOLVE TO EMBRACE TECHNOLOGY – IF YOU DON'T HAVE THE SKILLS, SOURCE THEM.**

2. **START SIMPLY AND EASILY – ALWAYS TRACKING YOUR RETURN ON INVESTMENT.**

3. **BUILD A SOUND BUSINESS CASE FOR THE BIG GAME CHANGERS.**

STEP

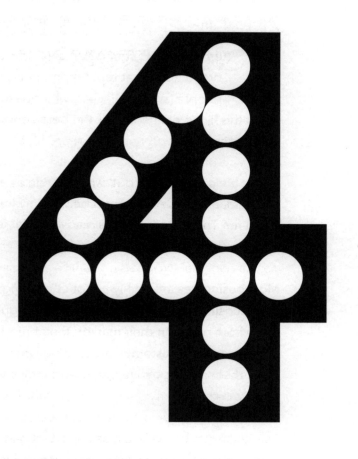

STEP 4
CREATING YOUR EMPLOYER BRAND

*T*o deliver and strengthen a world-class brand and great reputation through your people (and let's face it, who doesn't want to do this?), it's vital to attract the best people for your organisation.

These are people who 'get' what you do as a business, and understand and believe in what you stand for. These people are already sold (at least in part) on contributing to your success.

Most businesses are highly adept at creating their consumer brand; what it is that distinguishes them from others in their market, their brand promise to their customer, articulating what gives them a competitive edge. And they invest heavily in this.

The employer brand is just as important, yet many organisations do little more than pay it lip service. The vast majority of organisations will fully understand (and invest in) their consumer/product brand in terms of what is stands for; why people should buy it; what the consumer experience will be; what messages they want them to take on board; the emotional connection (for Coca-Cola, for example, this is about 'having a good time'; for Nike it's about 'winning' and so on).

However, many of the same organisations fail to define and communicate why people would want to work there, who will excel there, why they'd be attracted to the company and how this is communicated. You could say that the employer brand is the marketing strategy as applied to the people stuff. It goes beyond having attractive recruitment advertising or an appealing careers section on the website, although both of those will be part of it. And once you link it to your consumer brand, well, now we're talking...

A good, yet simple, example of this is Southwest Airlines, which recruits fun people in order to give the customer a fun experience. If you want to see this in action, put 'Southwest Airlines rapping safety information' into any search engine.

By thinking of your employees and prospective employees as 'consumers', it's possible to craft an employer brand which allows you to:

★ build your reputation as an organisation for which people want to work

★ attract the best, most appropriate, talent

★ strengthen relationships with existing and potential employees

★ enhance your consumer brand

★ ensure people view your company the way you want them to.

Whoever is responsible for the people stuff must therefore become a capable marketer (or work with their marketing department effectively). This applies as much to a multi-corporation as it does to a single-site local shop.

The employer brand stuff only works if it's aligned to your culture and you actually deliver on what you say you will do. Business is transparent and information flow is easy and fierce. Websites such as Glassdoor quite rightly ensure that organisations can no longer get away with selling 'the dream' to would-be recruits and then delivering something quite different.

In the same way that you wouldn't buy a mobile phone or a laptop without reading the reviews and asking your network, job seekers do their research too. If you're not a great company to work for, and fail to deliver on your brand promise, people will know.

As much thought should therefore go into managing your market reputation as an employer as it does into your marketing of products and services. When

marketing a new product, organisations spend shed-loads of time and money making sure consumers know about it and understand what it can do for them. This, in turn, creates a desire to buy.

THE EMPLOYER BRAND STUFF ONLY WORKS IF IT'S ALIGNED TO YOUR CULTURE AND YOU ACTUALLY DELIVER ON WHAT YOU SAY YOU WILL DO.

But relatively few businesses are putting even 10% of that resource into positioning themselves as a great place to work. Yet for those who place the same amount of importance on creating and managing employer reputation as managing their consumer brands, the results are powerful.

Just take a look at Virgin, John Lewis, Innocent and even McDonalds.

THE PEOPLE PROMISE

The employer brand starts with the EVP "the employee value proposition".

I like to call this your people promise: a statement of everything to do with each employee's experience throughout their life-cycle within the organisation.

In short, it's the answer to "what can I expect here?" and encapsulates things such as your mission, values, leadership, culture, benefits, progression and development opportunities. This isn't about investing in lots of great employee benefits or thousands of learning courses (you don't want to over-promise). Start simply by writing down what you offer now. Then find out what you might want/be able to add later. What would your people value?

Once you understand the importance of a well-defined people promise, and are able to articulate it to the organisation and deliver on it, you will have created significant competitive advantage. What's not to love?

You need to make your organisation a great place to work and shout about it. Only then will your promise shine out and the best talent come flocking. Well, actually, your people will do it for you.

Again, this reflects the importance of buy-in from the top. It has to feed through the entire organisation, starting from the owner, board, the CEO or MD. It is not just an 'HR initiative'. It's a way of life to be built upon, refined, updated, cosseted, loved and cherished.

Always keep it simple, of course…

Things you could include:

★ how things are done around here
(see STEP 2, culture and values)

★ the way people are led and managed

★ how communication works
(see STEP 5, internal communications)

★ commitment to development and
employee progression

★ reward and recognition

★ corporate social responsibility (CSR)
opportunities.

And so on. A well-crafted people promise will take
the heat off pay and benefits as the main motivators.

Put some simple measures in place so you can do
a 'before and after' comparison; a simple survey is
an obvious method. When you can clearly see the
value you are adding, it will keep you motivated (and
persuade any doubters) to carry on.

Always bear in mind that if the way you, or anyone
else within your organisation, leads and deals with
your people couldn't be comfortably reported on
the front page of a major newspaper, or as part of a

'back to the floor' TV reality show, you need to make some changes.

Remember, your people promise may well be a work in progress that evolves as you go along. Just be careful to enhance it instead of taking elements away unless they no longer work for you and your people. And once you know what your 'offer' is, you can set about communicating it, in the same way you would your product offer. So put a marketing plan in place, which is likely to include:

★ living up to the promise

★ leaders reinforcing key messages

★ updating your website: make the 'join us' section interesting and engaging (so many aren't) and make applying online simple and easy

★ using social media – get your message out there

★ cascading your message through internal and external networks and brand ambassadors.

Call in the marketers – they know how to do this stuff…

A 10-POINT PLAN TO SHAPE YOUR PEOPLE PROMISE:

1. Write down everything you offer now.

2. Consult your people about what they think and how well you deliver; ask them what could make it better.

3. Work out what's feasible now, later, never.

4. Craft your people promise.

5. Write it down, simply.

6. Market test it.

7. Communicate your promise very clearly, referencing point three.

8. Deliver on your promise.

9. Review and refine it.

10. Keep communicating it.

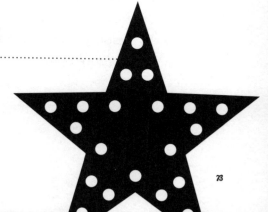

DON'T JUST TAKE IT FROM ME

CASE STUDY: INNOCENT

Drinks manufacturer Innocent is passionate about keeping alive a strong people-centric culture and linking this to its people promise.

★ It has a specific team in place to look after culture.

★ It recruits strictly in accordance with its values.

★ As well as being a great place to work, Innocent prides itself on a strong core of operational excellence.

★ It encourages consumers to come into its offices (or 'Fruit Towers'), where employees show people around.

Innocent proudly says: "You can't underestimate the power of working for a company you are genuinely proud of…"

Its people promise is: "Part pay/benefits + part culture/development."

IF YOU ONLY DO

three things:

1. **PUT EFFORT INTO BOTH YOUR EMPLOYER BRAND AND YOUR CONSUMER BRAND AND LINK THEM.**

2. **DELIVER ON A GREAT PEOPLE PROMISE AND MAKE SURE EVERYONE KNOWS IT.**

3. **KEEP THINGS SIMPLE AND BUILD – LOOK FOR THE QUICK WINS.**

Notes...

....

....

....

....

....

STEP

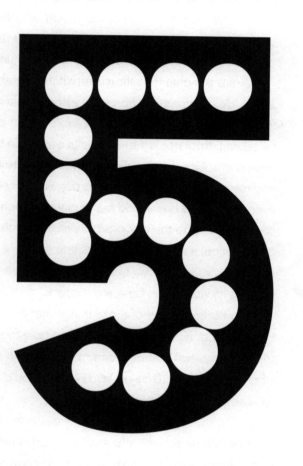

STEP 5
INTERNAL COMMUNICATIONS

*I*n the same way that your culture and values are the glue that sticks everything together, clear communication must also run as a thread through all that you do. It is not a subject than can be taken lightly, nor left to a handful of people to implement. Good internal comms is difficult to achieve and maintain, though it becomes considerably easier if everyone knows how to do it and plays their part. Great comms has to be the responsibility of everyone in the organisation; it's up to you to facilitate this.

Despite its vital role in business success, communication is one of those things that can always be improved. If you ask any employee how they'd rate their organisation's internal communication on a scale of one to 10 (with 10 being 'it's brilliant'), you'd be lucky to raise a five in most organisations.

We live in a world where everyone is bombarded with information 24/7; where business moves faster than ever before. While many companies put a lot of time and effort into communicating, so much of what is conveyed simply gets lost.

For instance, suppose you want to communicate a change in the structure of your IT team. You email it out. You put a revised organisational chart on your internal comms platform. You ask line managers to mention it in their next team briefings. Then three months later, people say they weren't informed. People fail to see the notice on the wall. The news update is lost among thousands of other emails. People leave meetings without clear understanding of what they've just been told and need to do next. They're so busy concentrating on their own stuff that what's happening somewhere else right at that time just gets 'deleted'. It's like throwing a tiny noodle into a huge plate of well-sauced spaghetti and expecting someone to find it when they're not all that hungry.

And this is not only happening within big business. In smaller organisations, particularly growing ones, people often believe that information will be picked up somehow 'by osmosis'. Or even where communication is done well and diligently, there's still so much to do and so much going on that messages are lost.

A SIMPLE 10-POINT PLAN TO ENHANCE YOUR INTERNAL COMMS:

1. Make every communication as clear and simple as possible – bullet points are a great tool for action-orientated communications like presentations and emails. Communicate the 'top line' signposting to the detail.

2. Teach people how to communicate effectively: introduce writing guides and so on (start with your leaders).

3. Make communication relevant to the recipient(s), using facts, examples and stories to explain what you mean.

4. Use uncomplicated, contemporary language.

5. Write it, edit it down, check it, run it by a colleague or if spoken, plan/practise it.

6. Ban unnecessary communication such as endless copying in of team members to emails; proceed on a 'need to know' basis.

7. Ensure people know where to find information centrally as and when they need it, for example via an intranet or shared folder in the cloud.

8. Never assume that if you've sent it out, people will take it in.

9. Use a variety of approaches to communicate an important message, repeating as necessary.

10. Check your people have understood by asking them about the communication in a one to one.

Less really is more.

There was a low-paid, part-time barman who had a simple idea relating to a different way of cleaning beer pipes. He'd held back from suggesting it, not wanting to overstep the mark. Then a new comms platform was launched, whereby one of the features was to submit ideas. He made his suggestion and when the change was rolled out across the company, it saved his employer £500K per year [see case study in STEP 3].

He'd assumed someone must have tried it already. Previously no one was ever asked for their opinions. Opening up two-way communications enabled him to make his simple-yet-brilliant suggestion.

OPEN COMMUNICATION CHANNELS

Imagine just communicating the important stuff and having less need for endless unnecessary communication because people were just getting on with things. They'd know where and how to find out what they needed as and when they needed it.

Create an environment in which communication channels are open and two-way; it's vital you are able to access the stuff from the grassroots.

The people who are 'doing the doing' know more about your organisation and its customers than you do. So instead of sitting in the board room deciding things, then expecting information to cascade downwards magically (through that often murky middle-management layer), get out there and involve people from the bottom up. This way, they will know what's going on and are more likely to buy into the decisions made.

THE PEOPLE WHO ARE "DOING THE DO" OFTEN HAVE THE BEST IDEAS – IDEAS THAT CAN BOOST SALES AND PROFITS OR SAVE YOU MONEY.

Since you (hopefully) employ adults rather than children, they deserve adult-to-adult relationships and an equal voice. This sounds obvious and some organisations are excelling in the way they communicate with their people. However, many are not.

The people who are 'doing the do' often have the best ideas – ideas that can boost sales and profits or save you money. Why wouldn't you want to access this valuable 'free' resource?

Communication is always going to be a work-in-progress, but is an essential component of your people formula. The good news is that as soon as people of influence start communicating effectively, others will follow – role model behaviours breed role model behaviours.

A QUICK NOTE ABOUT... MEETINGS

Meetings are one of the most popular methods for disseminating information, though very few are run effectively. Some people have meetings for meetings' sake - or worse; unproductive meetings that go on too long, bore everyone to death and achieve very little. There are people who love the sound of their own voices or just enjoy having a rant while chairing the session. Some people spend so much time trawling through past detail and conducting 'post mortems' of former strategies or events, they never get on to the good stuff – the future.

Hint: if you don't feel excited about going to a meeting, the other parties won't either. Do something about this. Conducted well, meetings can be dynamite (in a good way):

★ Decide what needs to be covered and the outcomes you would like to see – then plan a timed agenda (or better still, let go and ask one of the attendees to plan and chair the meeting – then you don't have to it and they'll feel more trusted and are highly likely do a great job).

★ Record action points only (what, who, when, what if – and possibly, though not necessarily – how).

PRESENTING TO A GROUP

Communication via a presentation provides leaders with a golden opportunity to engage a whole lot of people at the same time. Good times. Unfortunately, it is also so very easy to disengage and bore them. Bad times. It's therefore vital the right people are saying the right things at the right time, in a simple, clear and engaging way. If you know your stuff and can communicate it well, it is more likely the audience will be engaged, will interact and will take the required action as a result. Yet so many organisations mess this up; here are a few tips.

A SET OF 10 TIPS FOR PRESENTING TO GROUPS:

1. Get the timing right (when, pace and duration).

2. Think about the group – what will get members excited and interested (what's in it for them?) Talk their language, using stories and examples to which they'll relate.

3. Each person takes in information differently, be it verbally, visually or through feeling or doing. Cover all bases if you can.

4. If possible, keep to three main messages and expand on these as required (people will remember your three points and forget most of the rest) – sum up clearly.

5. Bin your notes, instead using prompt words on a card (or better still learn them) and talk from the heart instead (get someone in to teach you how).

6. Get the tone right, using humour if appropriate. For negative news, be frank and honest, yet kind and empathetic.

7. Use emotion. If you're excited sound that way; and smile; if you're conveying serious stuff, empathise.

8. Vary vocal tone and physical position (though avoid fidgeting about).

9. Make any visuals simple, appealing and visible from the back of the room (and never read them out verbatim).

10. Read the mood in the room – are people listening, nodding their heads (or otherwise)? Adapt your approach to keep them interested and on your side.

EMPLOYEE SURVEYS

Finding out what people think and feel is an effective first step towards being a great place to work and therefore becoming more productive, profitable and high performing. If you and your fellow leaders, managers and supervisors are interacting regularly with your people and have created trusting relationships with them, you'll know what they think. There are times, though, when you might want to take a 'snapshot' of how everyone feels about a range of issues – or perhaps one specific topic – and that's when employee surveys can come in handy.

Employee surveys do not replace dialogue – they should promote and support it. In smaller organisations, just ask people.

There is now a new breed of survey whereby instead of asking the same questions of everyone, respondents are first asked what's important to them in a ranked order and then score those aspects. This makes the feedback personal to the individual and highly relevant to the business – highly recommended by me!

Employee surveys not only find out what people think, they let people know that you care what they think – which is very important. This only works if you make a great job of doing something with the results.

Avoid long, boring surveys that are hard to fill in.

This 'spray and pray' approach is confusing for everyone and gives too much detailed data, which you're unlikely to have the time or resources to analyse and address fully.

EMPLOYEE SURVEYS NOT ONLY FIND OUT WHAT PEOPLE THINK, THEY LET PEOPLE KNOW THAT YOU CARE WHAT THEY THINK.

Make your survey visually attractive and on brand. Use pictures. Keep the language simple and contemporary. For best results, consult a professional – there's a science and art behind constructing smart questions.

YOU SHOULD ONLY EVER RUN A SURVEY IF:

★ you feel you're culturally ready to deal with this type of intervention

★ you're prepared to take the feedback on the chin, without recriminations (bearing in mind some of it might not be what you were expecting)

★ you're able to act on it, and for the things that can't change, you're willing to explain why honestly

★ you're prepared to communicate what you've learned and what you're going to do about it, in a transparent way

★ you're doing it to make real business improvements and not just tick a box (it happens).

DON'T JUST TAKE IT FROM ME

"Great employee engagement represents the involvement of everyone in the things that move a company forward. It is not a tick-box exercise or one way communication to staff. These types of communication don't drive engagement. It's about involving people and helping them understand that they contribute to the key objectives of the company and how the bigger company strategy relates to them. Engagement is not a distant thing – it is present and it is powerful.

"It is about making sure employees are connected. It's about making people see that there is more to their job than turning a handle. At EE, we have an

in-house social media system called Splash, where employees can chat and post updates. Here, our people come up with loads of great ideas and innovations. It's important to allow openness to encourage this level of engagement."

ROBERT PURDY, DIRECTOR OF IT, CUSTOMER MANAGEMENT AND DELIVERY, EE

"Our people are so central to the success of our business that engagement and our talent pipeline sits alongside profit and customer service in our list of priorities. We've digitised our talent management approach and created a business communications hub where people regularly record 'coffee chats'.

"In order to engage our millennials, many of our business areas have local Facebook groups and tell us we are making marked improvements in our communication. Our focus remains on people leadership, internal communication and social collaboration which is transforming our business."

MOIRA LAIRD, HR DIRECTOR, VALOR HOSPITALITY PARTNERS

IF YOU ONLY DO
three things:

1. EXPECT EVERYONE TO BE RESPONSIBLE FOR GOOD COMMUNICATION AND KNOW HOW TO DO IT.

2. CREATE 'FREEDOM WITHIN A FRAMEWORK' AND GET PEOPLE DECIDING FOR THEMSELVES.

3. THINK BEFORE YOU COMMUNICATE; KEEP IT SIMPLE.

Notes...

....

....

....

....

....

....

....

....

....

....

....

....

....

....

....

....

....

....

....

....

STEP

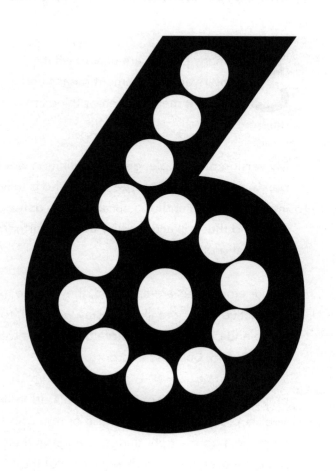

STEP 6
EMPLOYEE ENGAGEMENT – THE BIG 'E'

So many people are unsure what employee engagement means and maybe it means different things to different people.

My version of a simple, generic definition would be: "An engaged employee is one who is fully involved in, and enthusiastic about, his or her work and thus will act in a way that will further the organisation's interests."

If your employees are engaged, they will be more productive and more likely to stay with you, to thrive and progress – therefore they will deliver a better brand, business and bottom-line.

Employee engagement is directly related to the people promise. People promise or not, good employers do the right things to engage their people – even if they've never heard of the term 'employee engagement'. Having willing, enthusiastic and committed people simply makes good business sense. Yet according to Gallup, 13% of employees across the globe are engaged. In the US alone, Gallup calculates this costs the economy approximately $500bn every year.

EMPLOYEE ENGAGEMENT:

★ goes beyond motivation and job satisfaction

★ is involuntary and cannot be requested
   or demanded

★ is a state of mind whereby employer and
   employee understand and honour their
   commitments to one another

★ is brought about by the employees' desire to
   act in the best interests of work and colleagues

★ is brought about by delivery of the
   employer brand.

As with all important business aspects, what gets
measured gets done. There's much ambiguity around
measuring how engaged individuals feel. Happiness
scales are useful, though used in isolation are not a
reliable indicator. You really have to look at a range
of metrics and then compare them with business
results. A simple way of measuring engagement is to
find out by asking people how engaged they feel, or
running a one-off, or ongoing 'pulse' survey (as they
are sometimes known) in four areas:

1. Satisfaction – do people like it here, do they
   feel fulfilled, are they happy here, do they like
   coming to work?

ENGAGEMENT STARTS WAY BEFORE PEOPLE ACTUALLY START WORKING WITH YOU.

2. Feel-good factor – do they love their jobs, feel proud to be here and are enthusiastic about what the organisation stands for?

3. Staying power – how long will they stay, how happy do they feel to be part of this?

4. Advocacy – do they say positive things about you on social media and recommend you to their friends?

A COHESIVE, ONGOING EFFORT

Imagine employee engagement as a virtual bank account whereby every time something positive happens, a bitcoin is deposited. And vice versa – coins are removed when negative experiences arise. So employee engagement becomes an ongoing, cohesive effort by all concerned to 'keep people up there'.
Too many organisations rely on disparate initiatives to engage their people, and it just doesn't work. That's why Gallup's findings also tell us that 87% of employees do little more than just show up for work each day.

So think of it as a flow.

Engagement starts way before people actually start working with you. When someone hears about your organisation for the first time, if you've created a great place to work, then you'll clock up a few bitcoins.

Then someone sees a compelling and exciting job opportunity online and it encourages them to apply – another coin.

They research your company and read about your people promise, your values and the opportunities you offer. More coins...

A really helpful person, with a friendly voice, invites them over the phone to come in for interview. (Kerching!)

The interview inspires them and they really want to join you. (Kerching! Kerching!)

They come to a second interview and you give them feedback from their psychometric test (which they find really interesting and useful – even if they don't get the job). Also, you reimburse their travelling expenses. (Enough of the kerchings – the engagement value is mounting up).

They receive an exciting job offer from the friendly, enthusiastic voice (yet more coins). Of course, they accept the role.

And then – the wow factor – two days later, they receive a well thought-out induction plan full of rich experiences to allow them to get under the skin of their new organisation. They're sent the latest company news, asked to do some pre-work so they can hit the ground running, they're offered the opportunity to choose a 'settling in' buddy. You get the picture...

Or even better – they were invited to download an app containing all of the above information, as well as tips from colleagues on where to pick up the best coffee on the way to the office.

Then some of their new teammates drop them a welcome email or post on their Linked In profile or the company Facebook page....

And on it goes...

You invite your new recruit to next week's BBQ, cinema trip or whatever event is happening, or just to meet their colleagues ahead of day one.

Doing all of this should earn you a good few bitcoins... Imagine: if you didn't do any of this, what a huge opportunity you'd be missing...

And, of course, all your good work will be for nothing if the reality doesn't match up to the hype once they've started. Being accountable for people is a massive responsibility and should not be taken lightly. This is why employee engagement is not something 'done by HR'; it is the ongoing responsibility of everyone within the organisation.

Engagement isn't just about the first few days of an employee's experience with you. It is a journey, and as such, a continuous thing. It has to be something that's nurtured, stratagised and developed the whole time an individual is with you.

So having made good progress in engaging your people from day one, it's necessary to keep building on this, ensuring they are both enabled and empowered. It's great to engage them in the first 100 critical days (when people decide how long they will stay with you, if at all), you then have to keep it up.

This can be tough, but it is necessary. So make double sure that all line managers and other leaders are fully on board with clicking up the engagement bitcoins. It's a key part of the modern manager's role. In the same way that a restaurant is only as good as its latest meal, your company is only as good as its last touch point with the employee.

THE 10 THINGS ORGANISATION SHOULD ENSURE LEADERS, MANAGERS & OTHERS DO:

1. Ensure people are very clear about what's expected; both in terms of behaviour and work performance.

2. Agree goals, targets and what a good job 'looks like'. Agree how these will be measured and do it.

3. Set people up to suceed to get their confidence up.

4. Make sure people have the tools and knowledge to become productive as quickly as possible; and to address this fast if not.

5. Offer ongoing support and guidance.

6. Trust people, leaving them to get on with things; show people respect, respect difference.

7. Allow people to safely try new stuff (even if it fails).

8. Review progress, offer coaching for great performance.

9. Offer interesting and stretching challenges.

10. Generally take care of team members, setting them up to progress and contribute.

JUST BECAUSE PEOPLE HAVE BEEN AROUND FOR YEARS, THEY CAN'T BE TAKEN FOR GRANTED.

Engaging people when they join you is just the beginning. It's a ongoing 'labour of love'. If line-managers and others keep the dialogue open, they can keep track of 'what makes people tick' and therefore do the right things to keep on engaging them. People's lives and priorities change. This is why ongoing one-to-ones are so important.

And just because people have been around for years, they can't be taken for granted. It might be that, for someone who's competent within their role and doesn't have any aspiration to do something else, you'll have to become a little creative about engaging them by looking outside the main remit. One organisation I know offers 'extra curricular activities' such as Spanish lessons and cookery classes to ensure people stay involved and evolving.

Think about the whole employee life cycle as a continuous journey and consider all of the touch points (as you would with the customer journey) and how people could remain engaged throughout.

DON'T JUST TAKE IT FROM ME

"It's really important to have an engaged workforce. According to Towers Watson, organisations with high engagement levels enjoy 6% higher profit margins, and according to Kenexa, engaged workforces mean five times higher shareholder returns for their employers."

VLATKA HLUPIC, PROFESSOR OF BUSINESS AND MANAGEMENT, UNIVERSITY OF WESTMINSTER

"We are number one in our field for customer service in the UK – and we came from the bottom. We attached the objective to get to number one to our engagement strategy. People in the call centre were engaged with offering great customer service; tech support was engaged by making sure all the systems were in place to provide a great customer experience. We focused on this strategy from high level right down to day-to-day operations. We made sure all staff were aligned in this vision and it worked well."

ROBERT PURDY, DIRECTOR OF IT, CUSTOMER MANAGEMENT AND DELIVERY, EE

"You need to be clear and consistent when engaging either customers or colleagues. Before they join, we make it known to recruits that 'we want to have a relationship with you and make you a 'fan''. Therefore good employee engagement starts with an excellent recruitment team who have the ability to make people feel great about us, even if they don't get the job.

"Our recruitment team are so important because they need to find who can fit culturally and can do the job. At Metro Bank, we hire for attitude and look for what we describe as 'zest'. This 'zest' is a positive energy that's transferred to everyone. We therefore engage people right from the start, and in our recruiting days, we tell people that we're looking for the 'M Factor'.

"We explain from the very start that our people need to take responsibility for what it's like to work in their team. Yes we survey, yes we measure scores, but we're interested in what we can do for our colleagues to make this a better place to be. This creates empowerment and we encourage people, if they find a stupid rule, to challenge us, or tell us when something doesn't make sense.

"We encourage people to do the right things and treat people like adults. If you do this, then your people will use their initiative – a key sign of an engaged workforce."

DANIELLE HARMER, CHIEF PEOPLE OFFICER, METRO BANK

"Employee engagement is about getting all employees aligned and working towards a common purpose. As a huge football fan, it is that moment when the World Cup is about to kick-off and you can feel a buzz around the whole country. Anticipation, excitement, a bit of apprehension too. Everyone joined together in a shared vision, that sense of expectation. We are all clear on what the aim is and it's time to get out there and achieve. Together. While the football analogy ends there, the sense of belonging, community and desire to succeed and celebrate together - that is my definition of true engagement. "

ALAN MELLOR, HEAD OF EMPLOYEE ENGAGEMENT,
PENTLAND BRANDS

"Lots of companies measure engagement; we go beyond that as we prioritise engagement as a precursor to sales. I know that if team engagement is strong and I can see it living and breathing in the business, it tells me our sales results in three months' time will be equally as strong."

BRIAN MCCARTHY, MANAGING DIRECTOR,
VALOR HOSPITALITY PARTNERS

IF YOU ONLY DO
three things:

1. VIEW EMPLOYEE ENGAGEMENT AS A MARATHON NOT A SPRINT.

2. GET EVERYONE ON BOARD WITH THE 'VIRTUAL BANK'.

3. ENSURE OPERATIONS UNDERSTAND THE IMPORTANCE OF THEIR ROLE IN THIS.

Notes...

....

....

....

....

....

....

STEP

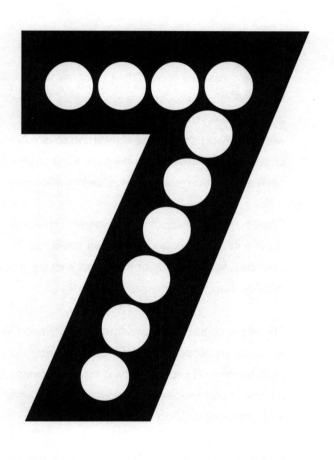

STEP 7

LOOKING AFTER HEALTH AND WEALTH

*a*lmost by definition, employers are responsible for their people's wealth. And all employers are responsible for health and wellbeing at work as well. It (almost) goes without saying that it's the right thing to do. And any organisation that wants to be a great place to work will have embraced health and wellbeing wholeheartedly.

Employees will expect it as a 'given'. However, we do live in complex and uncertain times, so it's not unknown for the budget in this area to be given less priority than that for other areas.

There are definite bottom-line benefits such as good levels of employee engagement and retention, high motivation and productivity, employee satisfaction, creativity and innovation, reduced absenteeism and less time lost dealing with conflict.

Assuming you have all the statutory health and safety requirements fully up to date, a physically-and-mentally healthy culture is likely to include all or some of the following:

★ general focus on, and promotion of, wellbeing

★ true equality across the organisation

★ support and empathy

★ respect

★ trust

★ shared values

★ consultation

★ fair treatment

★ positive environment

★ a safe and well-run place to work

★ good leadership

★ an attendance culture

★ healthy corporate social responsibility (CSR).

With team members who are able to:

★ drive their own progress

★ feel in control over their own role

★ benefit society

★ fulfill both personal and work goals

★ be healthy and energetic

★ understand how they fit into the big picture.

There's also increased focus on the employer ensuring employees are financially secure and knowledgeable. For example, making available financial and pensions advice rather than just handing people their pay slips and assuming they understand how best to use their incomes to safeguard their financial futures. Making available advice on how best to manage personal finances, and debt management, is especially important in light of the advent of pay-day loan companies, some of which charge interest rates of more than 1,500%, plus fees. (Boo, hiss).

You can see how more or less everything in this book would make a positive contribution to wellbeing at work. However, there are a few specifics you should address.

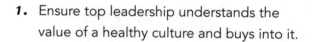

A 10-POINT PLAN FOR CREATING A WELLBEING CULTURE:

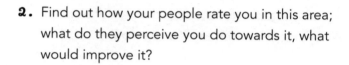

1. Ensure top leadership understands the value of a healthy culture and buys into it.

2. Find out how your people rate you in this area; what do they perceive you do towards it, what would improve it?

3. Review your work-life balance and financial education arrangements – challenge your business to do better.

4. Draw up your action plan (you might be surprised at what's uncovered and therefore have a lot, or a little, to do).

5. Build a supportive environment, in which leaders and managers commit fully to creating a wellbeing culture.

6. Work out logistics and priority order – better to tackle three things well than do lots of things poorly.

7. Communicate your intentions.

8. Run a pilot and evaluate this.

9. Deliver on your promises.

10. Monitor, evaluate, evolve.

Some lower investment items that contribute to wellbeing:

★ providing a pleasant working environment e.g. acceptable temperatures; acceptable lighting; comfortable desks; good decor; sufficient space; break-out areas and so on

★ making available healthy drinks and plenty of water

★ free fruit and healthy snacks

★ quiet room/chill-out zone

★ room for chatting and taking breaks

★ allowing use of headphones for people who are focusing on work in a noisy environment (or using 'do not disturb' signals such as flags)

★ making sure people take proper breaks and all of their holiday entitlement

★ allowing people to turn off email

★ encouraging exercise (even if it's just a walk round the block)

★ subsidised gym membership

★ in-chair office massage

★ time management
   sessions to help people
   control their workload

★ nutrition workshops

★ comfortable,
   supportive chairs

★ workplace assessment

> The behaviours of managers, leaders, employees the organisation as a whole all need to show that they're really on board with a 'wellbeing' culture or you may as well not make the effort in the first place. Leaders and managers have to 'walk the talk.'

★ buddy or employee counsellor

★ random acts of kindness such as buying
   team cakes or sending flowers to an
   unwell colleague

★ financial education workshops to help people
   take better control of their finances.

It's important to note that the value of the 'nice to haves' such as cool office décor and fun stuff will be lost if you fail to put in place the basic building blocks like treating people fairly and transparently and so on…

THE SCOURGE OF EMAIL

Email – love it or loathe it, this and the advent of multi-function devices such as smartphones, are largely responsible for the 'always on', 24/7 business

The Harris Interactive/ Everest College US Workplace Stress Survey *found that people's stress levels increase to 83% when using business email and to 92% when they're using an email and phone 'combo'. So it makes sense that a holiday should be just that – people need a proper break to relax, recharge, reinvigorate...*

culture that's developed here and in most other parts of the world. This wonderful connectivity was supposed to make life easier – and in many ways it does – yet it's also responsible for a great deal of workplace stress.

Combined with the 'cover your backside' tradition of copying in all and sundry to emails, traffic levels have become pretty unmanageable – unless you apply some email discipline. There's loads of stuff on the internet about how to do that, but here's one example you might not find:

What most people don't know is that it's possible to set up your email so that people who are away on holiday don't receive any messages, therefore avoiding holiday logging-on and a fit-to-burst inbox on their return. Instead, senders receive a message along the lines of:

"At X Co. we're able to have a proper break when we're on holiday, so your email won't be delivered to my inbox. If you'd prefer a response from me please resend on (date) or, if more immediate support is needed, please forward on to (colleague) or call the office on (no.). Many thanks for helping me to recharge."

Ok, so you'll probably have issues getting people to embrace such a change, but keep at it, it's so worth it. Not customer-centric? Surely customers today appreciate the benefits of working with those who come back from holiday fully refreshed, and are happy to deal with another competent person in their absence?

Adopting this seemingly small change can have dramatic results. It means that practically all of the internal traffic just 'goes away' and as long as colleagues are willing and able to deal with urgent stuff, service quality isn't affected. A rule can also be set up that allows emails with keywords in the subject box such as 'urgent' to be let through, and not deleted. In the unlikely event of an emergency, the business can also, of course, contact people by other means.

Not only do people enjoy stress-free holidays, they come back to a practically empty in-box. So, instead of having to spend two days trawling through the backlog, they can get on and be productive right away.

It's equally important to deal with other forms of stress and, again, I'll leave you to look that up.

A QUICK NOTE ABOUT...
BENEFITS THAT EXCITE AND ENTHUSE
How you reward and recognise your employees is something that should be led from the top – it

is not 'an HR initiative' - exciting benefits form a fundamental part of what you are as an organisation.

On the basis that people are individuals and should be treated as such, I'd recommend you look at some sort of flexible arrangement when it comes to benefits – one person might trade off work-life balance against pay; another might much prefer development opportunities to a Christmas hamper. There are web-enabled systems to help manage this if you're a large enough organisation, otherwise:

★ find out what sort of things would make a real difference to people's lives, make you a better place to work; stuff that people will really appreciate

★ work out what's feasible, or even better, task a group of employees to do this

★ get organised and deliver – consistently

★ continue communicating – openly and honestly

★ keep checking benefits are working for all parties.

Remember, it's much harder to take away than to give, so start simply and build as you go.

WHAT IS APPROPRIATE?

Just because you're into snowboarding, fast food or bringing your dog to work it doesn't mean everyone who works with you will be too. While it's important to think about the individual, it's also essential to make sure the benefits you offer don't offend or alienate anyone. You'll need to make sure what you offer is in line with your organisation, not only culturally but whether there's a fit with your brand, products and services, field of work. Find out what people would value – ask them – you might be surprised. Overall, it's a tricky balance, though done well, a great thing.

DON'T JUST TAKE IT FROM ME

CASE STUDY

E.ON is one of the world's largest investor-owned power and gas companies delivering services to around five million people in the UK. Its customer service centre based in Bedford, employs approximately 350 staff team members, and there are many other operational sites across the UK.

As one of the largest employers in Bedford, with an average employee age of 41, health and wellbeing is vital to the business to ensure the company is able to cope within the busy customer service environment. E.ON's employees' length of service averages 11 years, with a part-time/full-time split of 58% and 42% respectively.

E.ON currently supports its employee's health and wellbeing with:

★ a dedicated intranet supported by the HR and occupational teams

★ regular healthy advice updates via monthly newsletters

★ an employee assistance programme providing unlimited access to advice, information and coaching from health specialists, qualified counsellors and a free and confidential support service.

On top of this, E.ON added 'in-house' expertise to ensure appropriate support and access to local health services. The company invited volunteers with an interest in health to come forward as 'workplace health champions' to help support and sign-post staff within the customer service centre. Four individuals came forward and attended a one-day accredited no-cost training course through their local public health team, gaining a Royal Society of Public Health qualification in health improvement.

All the workplace health champions are given ongoing support by Nuffield NHS Trust and are fully trained in first aid and smoking cessation management. They are regularly updated through health and wellbeing training provided every four months and are equipped with the tools needed to address the needs of individuals confidentially, and where necessary, take a proactive approach to supporting colleagues.

Although there is a serious element to delivering health and wellbeing within the organisation, there is also a focus on having fun and supporting charities along the way. E.ON took part in the Movember campaign to raise awareness of the risks of male cancers, and in special fundraising days supporting Macmillan Cancer Support, the MS Society and other charities, including the opportunity to focus on physical activities to support its charity of the year – the NSPCC.

IF YOU ONLY DO
three things:

1. MAKE SURE TOP LEADERS BUY INTO, AND SUPPORT, YOUR WELLBEING CULTURE.

2. REVIEW YOUR OFFER AND EVOLVE IT.

3. GET EMAIL UNDER CONTROL.

Notes...

....

....

....

....

....

....

STEP

STEP 8
TALENT AND PERFORMANCE REVIEW

I'm on a mission to rid the world of the term 'talent pools', because everyone is talented in one way or another.

It's your job to make sure you find people whose talents fit your organisation, who can thrive there. And it's your job to uncover and harness the talents of all individuals as appropriate, rather than those of an elite few.

In short, you need to know:

★ who you have working with you

★ where they are now (in terms of career/ development, and also geographically)

★ how well they are performing

★ their talents

★ their aspirations (remembering they may well be very different from what you assume)

★ their potential in the context of your environment

★ how engaged they are

★ how ready they are for whatever's next

★ who could replace them when they move on.

There are all sorts of innovative tech tools to help you do this. It is vital that, as with any other area of the organisation, the people function can access the right tools to get the job done as quickly and easily as possible. However, many organisations, some of them sizeable, are still labouring with paper systems or just not getting to grips with this critical stuff at all.

You wouldn't process your accounts manually, so why put what is arguably your most important asset through a dull, tedious, over processed tick-box exercise around performance?

The talent review is, and should be, all about succession planning, creating a leadership pipeline and making sure you have the right people in the right roles, at the right time. This is exciting: it presents opportunity for your people. Don't let it get lost among the mundane performance 'chat'.

REVIEWS AND APPRAISALS

Some organisations are getting rid of the annual appraisal. Of course, managing performance and

One-to-one reviews are a real opportunity to develop a productive, professional relationship. As well as the business stuff, get to know each other as people, tell company stories, talk about personal interests, family or sport…whatever floats your boat. This will enable you to help 'grow the whole person' not just their work persona.

exchanging feedback should be an ongoing part of everyday business life. And systems should be put in place to make sure this happens.

However, I believe that it's also necessary to set aside some time for a more formal, forward-focused, big-picture career discussion at least once a year.

Business pressure and human nature will dictate that ongoing review sessions will end up being mostly about 'work stuff'; practical aspects, performance management and feedback. Yet in a fast-moving, volatile and uncertain climate, where change is the norm, to engage and retain talented people, businesses must manage aspirations fully and transparently.

It's surely a business priority to help people develop and progress towards their potential and expectations?

The solution is to back up ongoing feedback sessions with a robust, more formal career conversation away from the day-to-day. The focus will therefore evolve from backward-looking, small-picture, 'performance management' to forward-focused, big-picture career planning. Today's employee will both welcome and expect an honest two-way discussion about himself or herself in the context of the business and the future plans and aspirations of both.

ONGOING PERFORMANCE MANAGEMENT IS A POSITIVE OPPORTUNITY...

Sadly though, for many, the traditional appraisal is a negative, backward-looking experience. Performance must be managed – this is how people learn and grow – but it should be done on an ongoing basis, as part of daily business. Often it fails to happen due to a lack of the appropriate skills within line management: the sort of skills managers need for dealing with customers and others too; the ability to handle potentially difficult conversations, fairness, objectivity, thinking skills, negotiation and so on... and that is relatively easily remedied through a variety of development options. For example, through on-job coaching, taking on projects, working collaboratively with those who are strong in certain areas, through self-study (online or otherwise); or you may need to run some off-job sessions to work through issues and examples, helping people to reach their own conclusions.

Ongoing performance management is a positive opportunity to:

★ progress an individual's attitude, skills and knowledge

★ improve team performance

★ engage people

★ give positive feedback

★ say "thank you" for a job well done

★ show gratitude for discretionary effort

★ help people fulfill their contribution

★ discuss development

★ harness ideas and feedback

★ plan for the future

★ help clarify the way forward

★ re-motivate, re-invigorate and re-inspire.

THERE'S MUCH RESEARCH TO PROVE THAT PROGRESSION IS A TOP MOTIVATOR.

Reviews and appraisals are something people know they should do and sort of know how to do, but then always seem to fall off the bottom of their to-do lists. Managers almost universally dislike appraisal time and try to avoid it. They find appraisals time-consuming, daunting, with little value or tangible results. Part of the challenge is that people aren't managing performance and other issues as they go along, as described earlier.

The point of annual, or other formal, review is to have a rich one-to-one discussion generating productive and inspiring future-focused outcomes. These goals and other outcomes must be properly recorded and easily accessible, so they are regularly updated and reviewed throughout the year. This way, the review process becomes the responsibility of the individual, not his or her manager, and it can move from a standalone annual one-off exercise to an ongoing, fluid way of progressing.

There's much research to prove that progression is a top motivator. I'd go one step further and say it's a basic human need. Growing the whole person, rather than just developing them to deliver the needs of the business, will reap rewards. You can't grow people if you don't understand them and aren't able to treat each one as an individual.

SELF REVIEW

It's vital that people have an opportunity to review their own progress before meeting with their line manager. Both parties should do some planning and then come together to discuss the results. You can imagine how, with an online system, this would be easily to facilitate.

ROI from online talent management systems is derived from:

★ reduced recruitment costs (better succession planning)

★ more accurate development needs analysis

★ time savings

★ improved performance management

★ people driving their own progress

★ more focused, goal-orientated people

★ activity aligned to strategy

★ improved engagement and retention

★ enhanced productivity

★ greater trust and openness

★ increased feeling of ownership

★ people feeling invested in and more valued

★ ideas generated

★ decreased conflict/grievances

★ market reputation – more job applications.

And if you incorporate your employee opinion survey that's a cost saved too.

KEEPING IT SIMPLE

The important thing (and this is emerging as a key theme of this book) is to keep things simple, clear, and unambiguous. Remember, the point of the appraisal or review is to have a fantastically rich, future-focused conversation, not sweating the small stuff and box ticking.

During uncertain times, many organisations 'put off' performance management and talent review because they find the approach more difficult than when everything is going well. However, this is exactly when a rich and honest one-to-one review is most critical. Managers should be encouraged to continue holding reviews. In order to do so, your line managers need to be given extra support and empowered to be transparent.

Make sure they are up-to-date and informed about the latest company news or situation the business is facing, as well as coached in the skills that are required to communicate this, especially if the update is not going to be easy to give.

It may also be that managers do not feel they have the time to plan and carry out a one-to-one effectively. Or they may be feeling pretty down themselves and the will to listen to others is eroded. So make sure they are also given the opportunity to air their views and are really listened to.

No matter how tough the economy, or how foggy the future, people still need to have a chance to talk about their personal aspirations and progress. It's the role of business owners and leaders to ensure managers can make this happen and are not afraid to do so.

The success of the organisation may well depend on them.

Once the review process is in place and working, the hard work is done. A well-crafted system will provide everything you need to carry out a first class talent review, thus planning for future business needs, making the most of the talent you have in place and enabling the necessary development, recruitment and activity required.

A QUICK NOTE ABOUT...
SALARY REVIEWS

In uncertain times, it's no longer a given that the inflationary increase (or more) will happen every year. However, if you're able to get right important factors such as communication, leadership, progression, development and culture, pay becomes far less important. Top that with a sound recognition strategy and you can avoid money becoming an expensive substitute for a positive culture. Of course, being aware of market rate and making sure that people are able to maintain a decent living are key. Being the 'highest payer' isn't, though. Make sure that the reasons behind the outcomes of pay reviews are clearly communicated.

Some organisations link pay with performance and that's up to you. Pay reviews should be more about market rate and the cost of living to maintain a fair

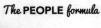

salary – reward and engagement through performance is a separate conversation. However, as the trends are firmly moving towards collaborative working, you'll want to consider team or company bonuses rather than offering incentives in a less cohesive manner which, in the long run, could prove divisive and counterproductive. The ideal situation is where people are rewarded when the organisation does well.

DON'T JUST TAKE IT FROM ME

"In many organisations performance management is still a separate exercise from people strategy that could be 'anti-engagement'. Performance management can be a formal and difficult process and performance circles and bell curves don't lead to positive engagement. I think it's inconsistent that soft and progressive HR strategies are not considered alongside performance management and it's important – albeit difficult – to find that balance. People should be developed as people in a cohesive way as fully rounded individuals. This is about more than sending people on courses."

ROBERT PURDY, DIRECTOR OF IT, CUSTOMER MANAGEMENT AND DELIVERY, EE

"Employers should look at all of these things holistically. People management, talent management, employee engagement and performance management are all part of the employee life cycle. Talent management done well, for example, is a key driver of employee engagement – as is leadership development. People don't leave businesses, they leave their managers…"

GARETH HUGHES, MANAGING DIRECTOR AND HEAD OF HR (EUROPE), ROYAL BANK OF CANADA CAPITAL MARKETS

IF YOU ONLY DO *three things:*

1. **COMBINE ONGOING PERFORMANCE MANAGEMENT WITH FORMAL FORWARD-FACING REVIEW.**

2. **MAKE THIS A POSITIVE EXPERIENCE FOR BOTH INDIVIDUAL AND ORGANISATION.**

3. **USE THE AVAILABLE TECHNOLOGY.**

STEP

STEP 9

LEADERSHIP AND PRODUCTIVITY

*l*eadership isn't just about the inspirational and visionary CEO. Leadership is about people.

To the person on the frontline, their manager is the leader, exemplifying what the company is all about. To have any chance at all of getting the people stuff right, organisations must create leaders at all levels. And if you don't have the resource to do this for everyone, start with those who directly influence the most people – which, for many – may well be the middle management layer.

According to *The Millennial Leadership Study* (Virtuali/Workplace Trends), while millennials aspire to lead, they define this leadership as "empowering others to succeed" and when asked what their biggest motivator was to be a leader, 43% said "empowering others", while only 5% said money and 1% said power. When asked about the type of leader they aspire to be, 63% chose "transformational", which means they seek to challenge and inspire their followers with a sense of purpose and excitement.

Millennials therefore want to work more collaboratively and be less accountable for personal

A total of 55% of millennials said that the most important leadership skill is the ability to build relationships, which 66% said was one of their strongest skills. MWhen asked what type of training would be most effective for their development as a leader, 68% said online classes and 53% said mentoring. Only 4% of millennials said university courses. Millennials prefer to have fewer managers: 83% of millennials said they would prefer to work for a company with fewer layers of management. Millennials say the biggest problem with their company's leaders is their (lack of) ability to develop others (39%) and communication (50%).

Source: The Millennial Leadership study, Virtuali/Workplace Trends

contribution. They are less concerned about being a leader as a position of power and status, and more about getting the job done. They wish to acquire and use strong leadership skills because they want to make a difference and have impact. This is very healthy and underpins the need to develop leadership capabilities at all levels from the get go.

This is why the elitism of a 'talent pool' is such a bad idea.

ROLE-MODEL BEHAVIOURS

If you think about leadership you will often see a cascade effect – great leadership breeds great leadership. Business owners and senior people in

PEOPLE EXPECT, AND HAVE A RIGHT TO, DECENT LEADERSHIP. AND THEY WILL DEMAND IT IF THEY DON'T RECEIVE IT.

companies need to make sure they are exemplifying the company culture and displaying role-model behaviours as well as excellent leadership qualities to ensure their managers – and the managers of the future – understand and exert what the company needs.

Weak managers used to be able to hide behind their status. These days, information flow is freer, expectations are higher and people aren't going to 'put up and shut up'. People expect, and have a right to, decent leadership. And they will demand it if they don't receive it. Or good people will leave you.

Of course, we all mess up sometimes, though that's about admitting it, dealing with it and moving on – this is actually an attractive leadership trait. If, hand on heart, your leaders (at all levels) aren't up to scratch, it's time to take action.

Developing leaders is a life-long process and something for which I believe the leader, or potential leader, should take their own responsibility. Yes, you can go off to Harvard, Tsinghua or London School of Economics and study leadership – and that's all great stuff – but not everyone has that opportunity and anyway I know from experience, it's only half the story.

During one enterprise conference at which I spoke in Singapore, the delegates seemed to fall into two fairly distinct groups. The entrepreneurs (many vastly wealthy, having built large, highly successful enterprises) with few or no qualifications other than the 'university of life'. Let's call them the As. And the Bs – highly educated and working within large corporations.

It was interesting to listen to them discussing what makes a successful organisation and how their leadership styles had impacted this. It transpired that many of the Bs were completely confounded by the approach to business of the As, where much was done on gut feeling and what you might term 'common sense', with relatively little analysis. That people would follow them towards their vision was not in question.

The Bs had become increasingly concerned about attracting and retaining great people and how many they were losing to more entrepreneurial

By developing appropriate role model behaviours across the organisation at all levels, you will not only be equipping future leaders, you'll be helping to 'grow the whole person' and dramatically improving productivity. People will be better equipped to work independently or in collaborative teams, there will be a need for fewer leaders in the traditional sense which will help you move to a more contemporary way of leading the workforce.

businesses. The As wondered how the Bs were ever able to get anything done! One commented: "By the time you'd analysed, evaluated and debated that opportunity and decided how you would deliver it, I'd already be doing it and, you would have lost out to me!" (Lots of laughter and a few uncomfortable shuffles.)

It made me consider how differently each had acquired their leadership skills, with many of the As learning in a practical way at their father's knee while many of the Bs were exceptionally well-qualified, but had learned the theory first and then put it into practice. Ideally you'd want a combination of theory and experience, which is why starting early, equipping everyone (managers or not) with basic leadership skills and experience in this area makes sense. Then top it off with the bigger stuff as and when you need to.

What makes a great leader will vary from organisation to organisation, culture to culture. This is why organisations need to define their core leadership principles. You can use the same process

CASE STUDY

One organisation that's crafted a comprehensive approach to growing leadership capability is award-winning business Lexington Catering (now part of Elior Group). It recruits carefully and views every employee as 'high potential'.

From a philosophy of 'nurturing all', Lexington Catering starts with cultural immersion via its Lex DNA programme, in which everyone must take part, working with DNA champions.

People progress through further stages and are given opportunities to nurture others so they not only pass on their skills, but also grow their own leadership abilities. As an example, they can be involved in mentoring others via apprentice and graduate schemes.

The Lexington Aspiring Leadership Programme has been created to develop the future leaders of their business and is accredited by the Institute of Leadership and Management. Formal learning is supported by practical assignments, challenges and experiences.

As a result, from an organisation with in excess of 700 employees, more than 40% of managers have been grown from within, many from entry-level roles.

as for defining and embedding values. Your leadership principles will then form a basis for development, assessment and review, continuous development.

This is why sending people on standard leadership programmes is not always the best use of investment in this area. Of course, leaders need basic skills such as communication, organisation and planning, decision making, proactivity and so on. However, they need to know how it is done in your organisation, not in someone else's. And unless you define this, who knows how leadership should work in your business? Omitting this vital step is how inconsistency happens.

This is particularly pertinent in light of the increase in collaborative working and flexible teams.

There are many ways to acquire these skills – from mentoring to self-study. So while you shouldn't completely discard classroom training, make it facilitated, tailored and involve real business issues. Those days of 'sheep-dipping' everyone in the same sessions are well and truly gone.

The most important thing is that leaders in the making must have access to this development on the way up – once they're there it's too late.

One of the simple daily self-assessment tools leaders use is to ask themselves: "If there were a leadership election today, would I win?"

A 10-POINT PLAN FOR GROWING YOUR OWN LEADERS:

1. Identify how leadership works within your organisation.

2. Define these core traits by behaviour – what great 'looks like'.

3. Embed these leadership principles across the leadership population.

4. Recruit new leaders against these criteria.

5. Assess leaders against these principles which will form their development plans.

6. Base core leadership development around what great 'looks like'.

7. Have robust talent management in place so succession planning is always up to date and you can identify future leaders.

8. Provide internal challenges and projects to test ability and inspire.

9. Access external secondments, mentoring and experiential learning to keep things fresh.

10. Check aspirations, development plans

and personal circumstances regularly –
things change.

....

It's necessary to import skills from time to time but it
makes for a healthy culture and better engagement if
people know they can fulfill their aspirations with you.

LEADERSHIP AND PRODUCTIVITY

When business people talk about productivity, they
often mean that employees need to work harder.
Perhaps this is because they believe people aren't
working hard enough already (or possibly as hard as
they perceive they did, or do, themselves).

The leader's role in productivity is to help people to
do their jobs more easily and therefore effectively.
People do generally want to succeed and, unless
they are disengaged and no longer care, they want
to put in a good performance. Good leaders know
this and therefore view getting rid of the unnecessary
stuff as a priority. This requires organisation and
thinking skills, and/or the ability to ask the right
questions, determine what needs to be done and
get someone else to do it. Leaders can cut through
the red tape by looking for the easy route to getting
things done.

It seems that it's human nature to complicate
things. This is apparently true of many business

environments. If every project, challenge or discussion were to start with "what are we setting out to achieve?" and "what's the simplest way we can reach the objective?", the outcomes would undoubtedly be better. It might take longer to do the thinking, but the execution would be faster (and probably cheaper). Communication would be clearer with less complexity to explain. By looking for the points of least resistance – the least complicated ways – and encouraging the team to ask "why are we doing this?" And "how could we make it simpler?", the leader can inspire the team to become more productive.

Good leaders can positively influence productivity by:

★   making things simple, easy and clear

★   providing purpose and meaning

★   accepting that people will have different capacities and work in different ways

★   deploying them in optimal ways

★   influencing behaviours

★   coaching and nurturing talent.

Overall, they become the conductor, not the principle violinist and certainly not the one who pounds the big bass drum.

DON'T JUST TAKE IT FROM ME

"We empower our staff to define problems in the marketplace and solve them. Our competition could be entrepreneurs working from home with no rules at all – we have to allow our staff this freedom so they can compete. We can't have a corporate free-for-all so there has to be some rigour and structure, but there is nothing more powerful than inclination, and we allow staff to have this."

TIM MORGAN, CEO, MINT DIGITAL

"We choose a group of high-potential, young employees, give them a boardroom challenge and then provide them with full access to our data feeds. They receive exposure to senior executives, participate in meetings at board level and have three months to place together a recommendation. This helps us continue to innovative and engage with our people, whilst developing their leadership careers at an early stage.

"We empower mid-level executives by bringing together a senior board from different countries to work on a specific project. We make sure they all meet (face-to-face) and discuss the challenge, then they work through the opportunities and financials before submitting their recommendation to the board.

"By doing this, we empower, engage and develop our

people while at the same time the company benefits from the different and shared views of how to meet our future challenges."

ALASTAIR PROCTOR, CHIEF HUMAN RESOURCES OFFICER, IPG MEDIABRANDS

"Being empowered is about being able to do what you need to do. Easy to say, hard to do for many leaders as their tendency is to control. Working on a truly empowered team feels like you're flying and you can't get more engaging than that!"

ISABEL NAIDOO, SENIOR VICE PRESIDENT HUMAN RESOURCES, FIS GLOBAL

IF YOU ONLY DO *three things:*

1. **DEFINE AND ARTICULATE HOW LEADERSHIP WORKS WITHIN YOUR ORGANISATION.**

2. **DEVELOP THE LEADERS OF THE FUTURE ON THE WAY UP, ALWAYS MANAGING ASPIRATIONS.**

3. **TASK LEADERS WITH MAKING IT EASY FOR PEOPLE TO DO WELL.**

STEP

STEP 10
SUCCESSION PLANNING

*a*s you will know by now, if you can successfully engage and retain good people, your organisation will be more productive, profitable and perform better.

But by how much?

Few organisations measure the true cost of attrition, i.e. how much is swiped off the bottom line every time a person leaves. My theory is that this is because it's just too terrifying a figure to think about. When I talk to business leaders about this, quite often they say: "It's just the way things are, it's a fact of corporate life, a cost of doing business", and have little aspiration to tackle in this area; there's always something more pressing. This is a really short-sighted approach.

Of course, some attrition is healthy – you can't keep everyone and you need to make room for new ideas. However, your objective must surely be to retain people for an optimal amount of time, instead of losing them before they've been able to make a good contribution. Many service organisations still lose upwards of 30% of their people each year (even if they don't admit it publicly). What a waste.

A 2014 study by Oxford Economics highlighted the cost of losing an employee. This concluded that there are two aspects to consider:

1. lost outputs
2. recruitment and settling in costs

Sector	Time taken to optimum productivity (weeks)	Cost per replacement employee (£)	Overall annual cost to the sector (£)
Legal	32	39,887	805m
Accountancy	32	39,230	580m
IT and tech	29	31,808	1,891m
Media and advertising	20	25,787	184m
Retail	23	20,114	673m

Source: Oxford Economics

Just to remind you, many organisations count the direct costs of replacing an employee but ignore the higher, indirect costs.

Indirect costs:
- Disruption to the business
- Reduced productivity/ output
- Lost opportunities/ revenue
- Knowledge loss
- Impact on customer relationships
- Reputation
- Motivation and morale
- Quality
- Continuity
- Increased competitor threat
- Knock on attrition

Direct costs:
- Recruitment
- Management time
- Interim temp cover
- Training

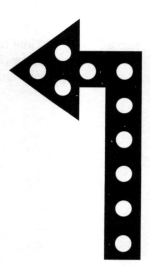

And if you want to use a more conservative figure in your calculations, in 2015 the Chartered Institute of Personnel and Development (CIPD) reported:

★ the average recruitment cost of filling a vacancy is £4,000 (£10,000 for a senior manager)

★ increasing to £6,125 when the associated labour turnover costs are included

★ if things fail to work out first time around you can expect to double these for the cost of rehiring.

The amount of activity and resource allocated to recruitment is disproportionate to that invested in engagement and retention. As an example, a company spending £500K per annum on recruitment that can't, or won't, find even 20% of this figure to invest in HR technology to transform engagement and retention.

Research shows that if people's aspirations were met, 70% of those who leave an organisation would stay. That's pretty major stuff and a compelling reason to sort this out.

Source: Purple Cubed

Some experts suggest that the costs go an awful lot further than this. Ultimately, if you're leaching people, you're leaching profits.

GENERATIONS Y AND Z

Millennials (those born after 1981), will account for one-third of the adult population by 2020 and 75% of the workforce by 2025 (Brookings).

There are various opinions about the exact dates for each generation; don't get too hung up on the dates – it's the difference in attitudes and characteristics that are important.

A word of caution, every generation will be influenced by later generations so it's not unusual to find, for example, a boomer who views the world in a similar way to a gen Y. That is great.

DEFINITIONS AND INFLUENCES

Generation	Born between	Also known as	Key influences
Generation Z:	1995 – 2012	Internet generation Gen I Digital natives	High-speed internet, smart phones, unlimited, instant access to media/all info
Generation Y:	1981 – 1994*	Millennials Echo boomers	Education, technology, parental input/ support, terrorism, social networks
Generation X:	1962 - 1980	Lost generation Latch-key kids	Divorce rate, working parents/ redundancies, crime rates, MTV, AIDs
Baby boomers:	1945 - 1961	The big bulge The Joneses	Post-war years, human rights, freedom, rock 'n roll, protests, travel

*The emergence of this new generation as a result of high-speed internet and its influences on a new generation alters the generally cited dates of gen Y and I have amended accordingly

The chart above is there for those who revert to type and endure conflict as a result.

While it's important not to generalise, each generational cohort will be influenced by the economic and environmental conditions within which they spend their formative years. As such there are some trends in attitude and behaviour:

CHARACTERISTICS

Baby boomer	Gen X	Gen Y	Gen Z (my predictions)
Live to work	Work to live	Work to fund lifestyle	Live then work. Workplace irrelevant, new ways of working
Long hours and dedication	Do the necessary and go home	Work/life balance, bored easily	Flexible, rapid progress, achievement without accountability
Motivated by prestige, perks, status	Motivated by change, freedom, respect, outputs	Motivated making a difference	Motivated by being heard, progress, change
Knowledge = power	'Show me what you know'	Ask many questions (generation 'why?")	Find own answers and offer solutions, value brands
Compliance, parent-child relationship with employer	Adult-to-adult relationships	Confidence to have adult-to-adult relationship	Offer opinions (often to the CEO); equality the norm
Know they've done a good job	Like regular feedback	Like immediate feedback	Constant feedback from variety of sources
Make own decisions without consultation	Take direction and then get on with it	Need constant collaboration/ direction	Need consultative approach, listen and be listened to as individual

Like structure and hierarchy	Have distain for authority and structure	Family values – require nurturing environment	Secure and loved, parental support, expect same at work
Like control	Hate being micro-managed	Need help with problem solving, like to share	Find info rather than thinking it through, expect top technology
Want to lead	Self-reliant, cynical	Don't want to lead	Don't like hierarchy
Resist change	Relish change	Flexibility	Super flexible, diversity the norm
Value experience	Assert individuality	Experience irrelevant	Creative use of technology to find out anything / everything
Competitive and resilient	Want to fix boomers' 'mistakes'	Take on tough, meaningful jobs	Manage outputs not inputs; want to do it their way
Parents said: "You can do anything"	"Stand on your own two feet"	"You're wonderful and brilliant at everything"	"You can be anything you want to be; whatever you do is ok with us"
Kept opinions to themselves	Shared their opinions	Think you want to know their opinions	Know you need to know their opinions
Write to me	Meet me	Conference call/ Skype me	Snapchat/Facetime me

THE 10 THINGS YOU NEED TO REMEMBER ABOUT MILLENNIALS:

1. They are socially conscious and are sceptics of big companies; they want to make an impact not only directly on the business but also on the world.

2. By 2015 already more than half of millennials have had three or more jobs.

3. They're digital natives, in many cases almost from birth – they're super-connected.

4. They value innovation in business on a par with profit – they want to be entrepreneurial.

5. Autocracy is their least favourite leadership trait; they question and reject traditional business practices.

6. They want to work digitally and independently yet also value collaboration.

7. They expect to be consulted and have their opinions respected and acted upon.

8. They expect to be rewarded according to performance and capability rather than age and experience.

9. They value EQ over IQ – knowledge is definitely no longer power because…

10 . ...they have access to every piece of information ever written in a click of a button (or swipe of a screen) and can therefore find out anything they need to know immediately.

STOP ASKING THAT INTERVIEWING QUESTION: "WHERE WILL YOU BE IN FIVE YEARS?"

All this challenges the way in which organisations plan for their future people needs.

When it comes to succession, this is an area that needs a clear plan. In days gone by, people were moved around like chess pieces and some were prepared to wait for 'dead men's shoes'. Now people have wised up and want to have their own aspirations met. For this, they need access to ways of driving their own progress, knowing where and what the opportunities are or could be. They need transparency.

Discussing aspirations and 'the next job' should start from day one. Stop asking that interviewing question: "Where will you be in five years?"

Who knows?

You could discuss people's ambitions and where they want to be next, though, and then talk about how you can help them to get there. This is great for engagement and, interestingly, is very likely to help you retain them longer-term.

CAREER WEBS AND NETWORKS

Regularly reviewing employees' aspirations and progress is essential. If it aligns with the business, it's important to ensure that wants, needs and desires are fulfilled. Be aware that not all talented people want 'promotion' – the career ladder or career path is an outdated notion.

Think about career webs and networks instead. So instead of a linear, upward approach to progression and 'promotion', someone might move sideways, say from marketing into HR. Or they might join a project team in another discipline for the experience even though in the traditional sense it wouldn't be seen as an 'advancement'.

And let's not forget the graduate whom, having slogged away to achieve a good modern languages degree, has abandoned her early aspirations of translation work to be welcomed enthusiastically into the world of luxury hotels

Harvard Professor Howard Stevenson, together with business leader, Eric Sinoway, explored the subject of workplace personalities further in order to identify employees who are good for organisational culture, and those who are hurting it. They categorised them as follows:

STARS: *the employees we all love – those who 'do the right thing' (i.e. perform well, the 'right way', in a manner that supports and builds the desired organisational culture).*

HIGH POTENTIALS: *those whose behaviour we value – who do things the right way but their skills need further maturation or enhancement. With development, time and support, these people are the future stars.*

ZOMBIES: *those who fail on both counts. Their behaviour is misaligned with the cultural aspirations of the organisation; their performance mediocre. They are the proverbial 'dead wood'. But their ability to inflict harm is mitigated by their lack of credibility. They don't add much, so the cultural damage they do is limited (and, naturally, these are the employees most organisations try to 'flush out').*

VAMPIRES: *the real threat. They perform well; however, they do so in a manner that is at cross-purposes with desired organisational culture. Because their functional performance is strong, they acquire power and influence. Over time, they also acquire followers: the zombies who share their different set of values and aspire to better performance.*

Soon, there's a small army of vampires and zombies attacking the stars, high potentials and leaders, eroding your culture a little every day. If you let them…

where she's succeeding and growing. Or the psychologists who, like fellow psychology graduates, acting legend Katharine Hepburn and *Playboy* magazine founder Hugh Hefner, decide to pursue a more 'creative' media career.

This flexibility of approach provides opportunities for businesses that are 'great places to work' to snap up the top talent.

So, because everything moves so much faster in century 21, it makes sense to review frequently as change can be rapid. You have to automate this, the data is faster, easier, more up-to-date and more accessible. It's impossible to keep track otherwise.

Also recommended is the use of succession- and business-planning techniques to identify:

★ roles likely to be created or freed up in the future

★ who is aspiring to change

★ what it will take to get them job ready

★ who is ready to take on a job

★ who is overdue a move

★ who is at risk of leaving

★ who should be managed out of their role
   or out of the business? The disengaged are
   mini-saboteurs threatening your business?
   If, despite all the circumstances and support
   being right someone is disengaged and not
   making a positive contribution, they need to be
   helped up or managed out before they have a
   detrimental effect on others.

People have a right to know where they are going.
They want to know when and how they will get
there and how they could be affected. An effective
way to do this is through employee-led regular
career reviews. This seems obvious though for so
many organisations this is a tick-box exercise or
doesn't happen regularly at all. Millennials will not
put up with that – they will find it elsewhere…

When managing aspirations:

★ be realistic

★ encourage people to drive their own progress

★ think strategically – avoid panic recruiting:

   ⇨ be very aware of future plans and needs

⇨ when someone leaves, review options before replacing

⇨ look internally first

DON'T JUST TAKE IT FROM ME

"The fact is that talented people want to choose what they do, where they do it and whom they do it for and with. So it's time to throw the traditional career ladder onto the bonfire; for in the future, things are going to be far less structured. This provides opportunities for the employer who sets out to be a 'great place to work'.

"My priority is to make sure that happens and then that we're fully aware of our people's aspirations, potential, capabilities and mobility. That way I can be ready for our expansion; I can make sure we have internal people in key roles rather than bringing in too many new people. This will constantly reinforce and uphold our culture and the delivery of our brand standards."

SEAN WHEELER, DIRECTOR OF PEOPLE DEVELOPMENT
PROJECT 1898

IF YOU ONLY DO *three things:*

1. **WORK OUT THE NUMBERS AND USE THEM TO SECURE INVESTMENT.**

2. **REGULARLY REVIEW PEOPLE'S PROGRESS AND ASPIRATIONS.**

3. **INVEST IN THE RIGHT TECHNOLOGY.**

Notes...

STEP

STEP 11
LEARNING AND DEVELOPMENT

*l*earning and development is a huge and ambiguous subject; there are countless methods for the transfer of knowledge and skills. It follows, therefore, that many organisations spend their HR budget in those areas. And, of course, acquiring the 'tools to do the job' is important. However, I believe that if you develop the right attitudes and behaviours, people will acquire the skills they need or come to you and ask for them.

Most of the traditional methods of knowledge/skills transfer were developed pre-internet. While no doubt some of this stuff still rings true (and/or has been adapted to meet current needs) there are easier ways to gain it than to sit in a classroom.

MILLENNIALS AND LEARNING

Millennials:

★ don't want to sit in a classroom

★ want you to tell them what you expect of them and how their progress will be measured

★ want to know what knowledge they'll need to

deliver – then they'll go off and acquire it

★ want coaching and mentoring as and when they need it

★ expect to use technology as a first port of call

★ love feedback and are open to finding out how they can 'do it better'

★ like simple, clear information and don't have patience to wade through swathes of information to find what they need

★ are used to visuals – stuff they can access on their phone while waiting for the bus.

Non-millennials generally like simple, clear visuals too. If people are highly engaged in their work, they're unlikely to want to take significant amounts of time out unless the experience is:

a) fantastic

b) life-changing

c) something they couldn't acquire just as easily on their phone

There are various statistics to show how little people actually retain from classroom training.

This will obviously depend on the circumstances, though will be significantly increased by the facilitator using a skilled approach to involve the learner, for example embedding the learning by working through a practical business problem together. One study concluded that people forgot as little as 0% of what they had been taught and remembered as much as 94%!

So if you're going down the classroom route – make it the very best quality possible. One-to-group development still has a role to play; for example for some leadership development or for specific subjects such as conflict management – where participants can learn from one another as well as the expert facilitator. It's vital, though, that learning is participant-led. This means that the facilitator is interacting with the learners at the start of the session or beforehand to find out a number of things about the topic they'll be tackling.

A GOOD FORMAT FOR KICKING OFF A SESSION

Discuss:

★ what group members' experiences are

★ what they know about this subject already

★ how they'd rate their competence

PUTTING PEOPLE TOGETHER WILL PROVIDE A STIMULATING AND INTERACTIVE SESSION, WHICH WILL ALLOW THEM TO SEE, HEAR AND EXPERIENCE THEIR LEARNING.

★ how it works for them within their role

★ what they'd like to improve

★ any specific examples they'd like to cover.

The subsequent session can then draw upon:

★ facilitator's own relevant knowledge of the subject

★ the knowledge and experiences of the group

★ current business issues that need to be fixed.

Putting people together will provide a stimulating and interactive session, which will allow them to see, hear and experience their learning.

It might be that you can reduce the amount of formal classroom L&D, reinvesting some (or all) of the savings in ensuring people's behaviours, attitudes and habits are aligned with your culture. And setting up some of the lower-cost, no-cost ways to provide development. As a result, you won't have such a hard time attempting to measure the ROI on your budget.

If you don't have a budget, look at some of the low-cost, no-cost resources (detailed on page 173), taking a little time out to structure how you and your people could use them to best effect.

Getting learning materials and formats right will partly be down to good communication and knowing where to go to find the information they need 'just in time'.

Herein lies a challenge.

If you Google 'how to…' there will be many different opinions and ways of doing things – who knows which is the best fit for your organisation? People could become very confused by all the options; one person could follow one approach, another something else entirely. So it makes sense to have a central resource of 'approved' company methods, perhaps via a cool internal 'wiki' type resource that stores information in a variety of forms for people to access easily, as and when they need to.

ATTITUDE

So much for skills, the really challenging part is attitude. Of course, if you hire for attitude and then develop the skills, that is far easier than trying to reprogramme someone's attitude.

Attitude is absolutely the responsibility of the individual. Make this clear at interview stage and again during induction. People need to be very clear that:

There are varying statistics, which put the percentage of people who learn by:

★ *seeing and reading at 45-65%*
★ *doing at 15 – 25%*
★ *hearing at 25 to 35%.*

This is why traditional 'chalk and talk' methods aren't particularly effective.

★ you want them to be happy with you and do well

★ if at any time they start to feel negative, or something is preventing them from fulfilling their commitment to you, they must raise it immediately so they can get help to resolve it as soon as possible

★ you expect positive, emotionally intelligent behaviours (which, in any case, you should be identifying at selection stage).

Of course, people don't always feel they can do this, so leaders need to listen to 'gut feel' to pick up on

> *A global head of people told me that to encourage her 400-strong HR department with the offer of coaching skills to enhance their roles and personal skills, she offered to foot the bill for 50% of any coaching development they undertook. Not one person took her up on this! Clearly people haven't yet woken up to the importance of these skills the business of the future.*

any unresolved conflict and/or negative behaviours.

Sometimes, leaders choose to ignore negative body language because they want to avoid conflict. In this case, work with them to understand that some conflict is healthy and show them how to deal with it. It's a key skill in this uncertain world. This is where assertiveness, support and empathy come in, as well as believing that people are basically good and want to do well.

SKILLS AND KNOWLEDGE

You'll be covering the basics during the induction period. This might be achieved through one-to-one work with a colleague or by more formal means. The important thing is to avoid 'sheep-dipping' people through the same skills-based learning. Find out what they know and fill in the gaps. By auditing skills against the requirements of the role, individual development plans can be created for each individual. Then it must become their responsibility to drive and complete the plan. This is very important. Technology is a great help in enabling everyone to keep track.

You'll need to make sure resources are available. People learn in different ways, therefore learning plans have to be different. If they are attending classroom sessions, there will need to be a mix of learning styles provided. If they are learning on an individual basis, the great thing is that you can vary the ways in which they learn. Here are some options – as you will see, many of these are 'low cost', or 'no cost' and may therefore, as mentioned previously, be preferable to traditional learning and development programmes when it comes to skills transfer:

★ reading books and journals (in-house learning library, virtual or otherwise)

★ intranet or internal 'wiki'

★ textbooks and technical guides

★ internet search – there's loads of free stuff out there

★ learning groups

★ podcasts

★ webinars

★ online learning (though traditional elearning is in decline with low take-up)

★ distance learning

★ in-house guides and other learning resources

★ professional factsheets

★ job swaps

★ secondments

★ work shadowing

★ projects

★ experiences such as competitor visit

★ interviewing colleagues

★ coaching

★ mentoring (a fantastic and definitely under-exploited way to learn).

Whatever the delivery method, learning should be:

★ appropriate for the individual

★ appropriate for the role

★ planned

* discussed beforehand
  to agree goals
  and outcomes

* well executed

* reviewed and outcomes
  checked both after the
  learning and again later to
  track the business benefit.

> *Giving people a trained
> buddy or mentor is a
> good way to ensure
> issues are dealt with
> quickly and outside the
> management structure
> (generally the best
> way for all).*

THE ART OF MENTORING

Mentoring is nothing new. To keep things simple,
mentoring is where one person with more
experience, knowledge or specialist expertise
guides another. It is a wonderful, largely untapped,
resource for learning and passing on all sorts of
good stuff.

It's not so much about occasional advice, but a
relationship, which builds over time (either ongoing
or for a set period). Ideally, both parties will learn from
each other. It is different form coaching. A coach is
normally a paid professional, whereas a mentor is
usually free. A coach works with an individual or group
to identify a specific goal or goals and frames the
discussion so as to identify how these goals can be
reached. The coach will not necessarily have relevant,
specific knowledge and experience.

It does make complete sense to equip your leaders, future or otherwise, with good coaching skills.

People might use different mentors at different times. For example, when starting in a new role, they might have a buddy mentor to help them settle in and learn the ropes. Or someone on a fast-track leadership programme might be mentored by a senior leader.

The important thing is to figure out how mentoring will work in your organisation. You might even invest in some clever software to help you manage it.

THE 10 TOP TIPS FOR MENTORS

1. Only commit to the responsibility of becoming a mentor if you are serious about it.

2. Build rapport towards a confidential relationship in which trust is key.

3. Do what you say you will, never over-promise and always follow up.

4. Believe in your mentee.

5. Ask great questions – and allow people to ask you 'stupid' ones.

6. Listen well.

7. Be patient and kind.

8. Be a role model, always.

9. You might not have all the answers, so work through the options.

10. Remember your mentee is not you and times change; there's more than one way to do something.

I find the mentor often learns as much from the mentee as the reverse. This is very desirable and equitable arrangement and is why there must be a trusting, equal and respectful relationship.

DON'T JUST TAKE IT FROM ME

"Our five-module in-house academy supports an individual's development throughout their career journey within Dorchester Collection. All employees, regardless of level, complete the engage and core modules, after which, learning reflects their individual role. The modules are set; however each property has the freedom to interpret them, and offer supporting development.

"We support this by hosting global and departmental quarterly and annual forums in addition to monthly L&D video-conferencing. This ensures people know how to access learning and provides us with feedback.

"Our L&D is respected as a direct influence on the profitability of the business. With careful consideration, aligned to business strategy, L&D can be the lynchpin for growth."

EUGENIO PIRRI, VICE PRESIDENT PEOPLE AND ORGANISATIONAL DEVELOPMENT, DORCHESTER COLLECTION

"Employees who are empowered, feel they have the support to lead and innovate. They have the tools in place to do the best job they possibly can, and vitally, they have the freedom of being allowed to fail. They are rewarded for collaborating and contributing to new ideas."

GARETH HUGHES, MANAGING DIRECTOR AND HEAD OF HR (EUROPE), ROYAL BANK OF CANADA CAPITAL MARKETS

"Learning and development, like engagement, can be embedded in the DNA of the organisation. Formal learning is important, but equally, it has to be in the culture of the business. Leaders could encourage their people to self-organise their own learning via the intranet and social media, develop their own learning groups and share knowledge."

VLATKA HLUPIC, PROFESSOR OF BUSINESS AND MANAGEMENT, UNIVERSITY OF WESTMINSTER

"Line managers drive engagement, the need
to link L&D and engagement is therefore huge.
It's something I would like to see more of. It seems
that many organisations partner engagement and
communications, I would rather there were a shift to an
engagement/L&D and communications relationship."

ALAN MELLOR, HEAD OF EMPLOYEE ENGAGEMENT,
PENTLAND BRANDS

"There's no better learning than the challenge when
on-the-job and all our feedback suggests that.
However, we also recognise that the majority of our
people are young and gen Y are interested in how
to learn, where to learn and in shaping their careers.
Because of this, and the demographics of our people,
a lot of our engagement is driven with learning and
development in mind."

ALASTAIR PROCTOR, CHIEF HUMAN RESOURCES OFFICER,
IPG MEDIABRANDS

"If you're engaging with your people and you tell
them you invest in people, they ask what training is
available, and your reply is that there isn't any or that it's
limited, then you lose all credibility and they disengage.
But if you say you invest in people and here are the
three-to-four courses a year that they'll be going on
as a minimum, now they believe you. So learning and
development is an essential part of how you engage
and support your people."

DANIELLE HARMER, CHIEF PEOPLE OFFICER,

IF YOU ONLY DO

three things:

1. **GIVE ATTITUDE PRIORITY OVER SKILLS.**

2. **USE LEARNING THAT'S APPROPRIATE TO THE INDIVIDUAL.**

3. **OPTIMISE THE USE OF THE BEST OF LOW-COST/NO-COST METHODS, BACKED UP WITH EXPERTS IN THE CLASSROOM FOR CERTAIN TOPICS.**

Notes...

....

....

....

....

....

STEP

12

STEP 12

EMBEDDING SERVICE EXCELLENCE

hatever you're selling, making, delivering or doing, there is likely to be an element of service. There's some great service in this world; and some that is, frankly, appalling. The challenge is significant, since customers and consumers want bigger, better, cooler, faster, more 'wow'. And there are competitor organisations chomping at the bit to give it to them.
There is clear alignment between employee engagement and customer satisfaction.

Therefore, if you want to achieve lasting results that will keep evolving, adapting and improving over time, it cannot simply be 'trained' in or 'road-showed'. You can design as many customer charters you like; they will only be effective if the people delivering care, believe and want to do it. As with your values, embedding service is not any sort of 'initiative', it is an ongoing culture thing.

It is important to have happy, engaged people giving service on the basis that they care about the organisation and the people to whom they are providing your service. This is why it's important to deal with the disengaged. You can show people the 'how' time and time again, but if they don't care or they don't understand the 'why' then you're not going to get the required result. This is because they are adults with their own values, opinions, circumstances and aspirations. These need to be aligned with yours for this to work.

It's also very important that people are properly enabled and empowered to give good service. Assuming you employ the right people, they need to be trusted to do what it takes to make the customer happy. For this to work, you will need a broad framework of 'non-negotiables' within which it is possible for service people to use their judgement as to what is required to meet individual needs (yep – customers are not all identical).

If you still have them, please throw out the rigid tomes of 'SOPs' (standard operating procedures) dealing with every eventuality – it's impossible to keep up (and no-one reads them anyway). Instead, embed a service culture (which is harder to do, but actually works – generally with stellar results).

DESIGNING YOUR SERVICE CULTURE

Once you have the right people in place, you can set about designing your service culture. It stands to reason that the people who know most about your customers are the people who serve them every day. So it follows that they should be involved from the get go. This is not a time for the L&D department to

FIND OUT WHO IS GIVING GREAT SERVICE, WHO LIVES YOUR VALUES AND COULD BE VIEWED AS A SERVICE ROLE MODEL. MAKE A LIST OF THESE PEOPLE.

put a programme together and train it in. Nor is it a time to bring in some experts to tell you and your teams how to do 'customer service'.

This is going to need very careful planning and super-competent facilitation and that's where your L&D department and/or external expertise comes in.

Find out who is giving great service, who lives your values and could be viewed as a service role model. Make a list of these people. This is just as likely to be Stevie in the post room as it is your head of client services.

Then ask for volunteers to work on shaping your 'service of the future'. Hopefully there will be some people who appear on your previously written list. Select a diverse group, including as many junior-level employees as possible. This is great development for them and you will receive fantastic buy-in and loyalty from their involvement. Free up some of their time so they can contribute without worrying that their job or colleagues will suffer.

Use great facilitation to enable volunteers to explore how service works within your organisation; the good, the bad and the ugly. And where they'd like to take it. This will enable them (not you) to work out how it can be delivered. They'll use this information to work out your non-negotiables framework. This is complex stuff and needs to be fully explored in all of its aspects.

Once leadership is on-board and prepared to give people the freedom (within your framework) to deliver, you can set about making it happen.

SERVICE CHAMPIONS

Ask for members of the group and others to volunteer as service champions. Teach these champions, and all managers, how to facilitate subsequent sessions and conversations around service improvement. This is to enable different customer groups, situations and so forth to be explored within the context of your service culture so that people have the time to work out how they can do the best job possible.

During these sessions, all the barriers to great service will be uncovered – you have to be ready and willing to deal with them.

Once this has been done, you'll obviously be looking at your metrics (e.g. net promoter score) and adjusting as required. From then on, it's an ongoing process as new people join, your service champions come and go and, crucially, business needs change.

This approach enables you to pick up on subtle changes and potential pitfalls before they grow.

Your people on the ground are your greatest service asset so use them…

A 10-POINT PLAN FOR EMBEDDING A SERVICE CULTURE

1. Employ the right people, ensuring your values are embedded.

2. Identify who your customers are.

3. Identify service champions to lead this (bottom-up approach).

4. Map the customer journey.

5. Use service people to design 'how service works here' (needs great facilitation).

6. Establish a clear framework of service non-negotiables.

7. Ensure leadership is on-board and role models for service.

8. Develop managers, champions and others to support, redesign, listen and act.

9. Use champions and service people to work with others on how they'll deliver (it's a virtuous circle).

10. Publicise great stories and examples of success.

A QUICK NOTE ABOUT... COMPLAINTS

Apparently, some organisations have target limits for the number of complaints received. All complaints should be welcomed and swiftly and adeptly dealt with. That old adage about unhappy customers telling 10 people can be completely reversed if you handle it well. A complaint is an opportunity to create an advocate. If they tell 16 people how well you dealt with their issue, then great. We're all going to mess up from time to time, that's life; people expect it. Your job is to ensure its handled with grace, to business advantage.

DON'T JUST TAKE IT FROM ME

CASE STUDY: DORCHESTER COLLECTION

Dorchester Collection won the coveted UK Customer Experience Award, 2015; judged to provide the best customer service in its sector. Eugenio Pirri, vice president of people and organisational development explains how…

"For any service business, the talent, skills and engagement of its people provide competitive advantage. Things like how warm the welcome was, whether genuine care and interest was expressed, were people working together seamlessly and did the guest leave feeling appreciated; combine to create what we define as the ultimate guest experience.

"It is our mission and focus to deliver this level of experience; better-than-world-class guest service, consistently. It's no surprise then that the previously mentioned behaviours are our guest engagement key drivers.

"L&D is much more than a tick box exercise. When L&D strategies are designed with employees, customers and owners in mind, the benefits are significant.

"Our long-term L&D strategy is focused on increasing engagement and retention; up-skilling

high potential individuals; and developing creative learning innovations to enhance guest experience.

"Guest engagement is measured through clear, physical, functional and emotional drivers such as experiencing seamless processes; improving a guest's life and working as a team.

"It is vital that people are appropriately skilled, developed, engaged and motivated throughout their employee journey. What's more, if we are truly to deliver exceptional service, this development must be driven by our guests. This is why all the development initiatives we undertake have to have a positive impact on both guest engagement and the bottom-line.

"For example, guest engagement scores highlighted a mismatch between guest complaints and employee response. Our people were not fully engaged in complaint handling and therefore treated the complaint as a request rather than something requiring resolution.

"As a result, we launched 'ProMisses' – problems and missed expectations – to solve guest issues. Aligned to this was learning through the academy; enabling skills and confidence to take initiative when handling complaints.

"By taking this approach to customer service, our guest engagement drivers have increased significantly; driving additional revenue and savings."

IF YOU ONLY DO

three things:

1. VIEW SERVICE AS CULTURAL.

2. USE THE PEOPLE WHO KNOW BEST TO DESIGN AND DELIVER.

3. AS IT'S AN EVOLVING JOURNEY, BE PREPARED TO INVEST YEAR ON YEAR.

Notes...

....

....

....

....

....

....

....

....

....

....

....

....

....

....

....

Part three

CRAFTING YOUR 12-STEP PLAN

T he trouble with business books is that while you're reading them, you're inspired, have loads of great ideas and even greater intentions.

Then you close the book, go back into the day-to-day running of your business and nothing really changes at all. However, if you didn't feel the 'people stuff' in your organisation could do with a little help, you wouldn't have bothered to read this in the first place. So, here's a final piece of 'ammunition' for you.

HUMAN CAPITAL MEASURES

Investors have finally begun to embrace, and place importance on, human capital measures. This means that if you get them in place you'll be ahead of the curve. Go in there and show them before they ask!

Before you rush off and go into potential 'analysis paralysis', remember that simple is better because it gets done. Look at the things you already measure and the stuff you'd like to measure. Temper this with the ease of doing it over a long period of time.

Investors don't really care about your KPIs, they want hard business metrics. There's no point going on about your five-point drop in labour turnover if you don't explain what this means in direct business terms. You have to think like investor, CEO and CFO rolled into one (as well as doing your day job).

Sadly, some HR is still a little on the back foot when it comes to being business-savvy, so be prepared for the tough questions and to talk investors' language for example .

"As investors we are there to hold companies to account and encourage good practice. We are looking for a happy, productive workforce – what data do you have that reflects that?"

Leon Kahmi, Head of Responsibility, Hermes

You'll need to know the numbers around things such as the make-up of your workforce, how stable it is, capabilities, succession plans, engagement metrics, productivity...and how all of this relates to turnover and profitability.

All of this says it's time to make a start on implementing the people formula...

A QUICK NOTE ABOUT...
ANALYTICS

The discussion about measuring the effects of HR is nothing new, though with the advent of big data, people are beginning to do it. Put simply, it's important to measure what you do in order to prove the value of various investments to the organisation.

And it's really important to be able to access information that will allow you to predict trends in order make key strategic and other decisions. Many people are worrying about how all this is going to happen and it goes without saying that investing in technology is the way to go. However, a word of caution: resist the urge to measure anything and everything. You simply won't have time to think it all through. Instead, decide on a few critical measures and, as with so much in this book, start small and simple. For example, you could kick off by tracking employee engagement scores and then map them against key business results such as profitability and productivity.

The important thing is to start putting this in place now…

A 10-POINT PLAN FOR USING THIS BOOK:

1. Familiarise yourself with the introductory sections, so the 'WHY' is first and foremost in your mind.

2. Assess your organisation against each of the 12 steps.

3. Put them in priority order – what requires the most attention?

4. Work out likely cost-benefit analysis for each.

5. Reprioritise by fastest results for lowest investment.

6. Try some of the simpler stuff for which you won't need to find much budget. Monitor the results.

7. Work on your master plan – this is a journey with many milestones.

8. Remember that some steps naturally support others, so think of practical examples and likely scenarios.

9. Work out the who, what, when and how you'll measure it.

10. Embark upon your journey.

GOOD

LUCK!

OH – AND DON'T JUST TAKE IT FROM ME

"At an individual level, good HR professionals become apathetic in an organisation where they are suppressed, whereas great HR professionals challenge the status quo and push for change – if the business doesn't respond, they will move on and the organisation they leave behind begins the cycle once more.

"A leader that understands the value of HR is an inspiration, he or she will accept challenge from the function but will be pragmatic enough to push back when HR initiatives do not deliver commercial value."

ALAN MELLOR, HEAD OF EMPLOYEE ENGAGEMENT, PENTLAND BRANDS

"Strategy and engagement are everyone's responsibility not just HR's. HR, to me, is a type of style in how we run the business with all your people, bringing them onside. On a practical point, you also learn more from people at the coal face and it's the simple stuff that matters. It's fundamentally important that you engage with your people at every level and get rid of the layers of bureaucracy, because when feedback is provided

through layers it's often sanitised by the time it reaches the top."

CLIVE JACOBS, CHAIRMAN, JACOBS MEDIA

"The UK has a wealth of talent across any discipline you can think of, all supported by hard-working and bright HR teams across multiple organisations, so in many ways, UK HR is enabling the economy to compete. However, if we are slow to embrace new ways of working then we could be holding the UK back. Think of all the data we are amassing HR functions across the country that is lying dormant. What impact could we have if we put it to work?"

ISABEL NAIDOO, VICE PRESIDENT HUMAN RESOURCES, FIS GLOBAL

"In our company, we don't have an HR department, so people strategy comes from the culture. But I have been thinking on the topic of empowerment; that HR departments, in fact also need to be empowered. In too many companies, they are wheeled out to solve problems and deal with administration. Imagine if HR's role was purely to create a place where people wanted to work?

"HR departments are keen to do this, but it would take a brave corporate to let them. I think HR should be the heartbeat of innovation. And I would put money on engagement being a vital, front-of-house strategy in all businesses in 20 years…"

TIM MORGAN, CEO, MINT DIGITAL

IF YOU ONLY DO

three things:

FROM THIS <u>ENTIRE</u> BOOK:

1. **SORT OUT THE CULTURE AND VALUES STUFF.**

2. **MAKE SURE YOU HAVE LEADERSHIP BUY-IN AT THE HIGHEST LEVELS.**

3. **INVEST IN TECHNOLOGY THAT WILL MAKE YOUR JOB EASY.**

Notes...

....

....

....

....

....

ABOUT THE AUTHOR

Jane Sunley is a CEO, celebrated author, lecturer, speaker and mentor as well as an established and renowned authority on 'all things people'.

Following a career as a business leader within the hospitality industry, the root of her pragmatic, real-world approach, Jane co-founded a successful specialist recruitment company which she exited in 2001.

Having realised that if someone could help companies to become a great place to work, there wouldn't be such a crisis over 'the talent war', she formed learnpurple which, in line with its expanded remit, rebranded as Purple Cubed, early in 2013. The company, which is on a mission to show the world just how to engage its people, through award-winning software plus expertise, has won many awards and accolades including UK's Best HR Consultancy (CIPD 2014).

Jane is a best-selling author having written *Purple your People: the secrets to inspired, happy, more profitable people* (Crimson) in 2001and *It's Never OK to Kiss The Interviewer - and other secrets to surviving, thriving and high-fiving at work* (LID) in 2003. In 2014 she was chosen from over 1600 authors to contribute to *20/20 – 20 great lists by 20 outstanding business thinkers* (LID).

She is a non-executive director and a visiting fellow at two UK universities as well as speaking and writing extensively on the subject of people and HR.

TWEET ME:
@janesunley

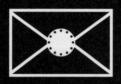

EMAIL ME:
jane@purplecubed.com

AND, IF YOU'RE FEELING GENEROUS WRITE ME A REVIEW ON AMAZON...